HAPPY FAMILIES

Bringing Up Children In A Christian Home

By the same author:

THROUGH THE YEAR WITH DAVID WATSON (ed.)

HAPPY FAMILIES

Bringing Up Children
In A Christian Home

by

Jean Watson

HODDER AND STOUGHTON
LONDON   SYDNEY   AUCKLAND   TORONTO

British Library Cataloguing in Publication Data

Watson, Jean, 1936–
   Happy families. – (Hodder Christian paperback)
   1. Family – Religious life
   I. Title
   261.8'3585   BV4526.2

 ISBN 0 340 32465 1

Contents

Introduction

The voice on the telephone was that of a wise and trusted friend, but I was shaking my head as I listened to it. I had been planning to write a certain book but he was saying, 'The publishers wondered whether it would be better for you to postpone the original idea, and do one instead on bringing up children in a Christian family.'

'Oh, no!' I cut in. 'I've got far too much to learn. Wait till I'm a grandmother.'

'When you're a grandmother,' he replied, 'you'll be too far removed from the situation to write relevantly: you'll write like a grandmother and not like a mother.'

'Listen,' I urged. 'Before I had children I had visions of being the perfect mother, but reality came as a very rude shock indeed.'

'What a perfect opening for the book!' he retorted.

That was more than a year ago, and now the book is a reality, thanks to the prayer, support and help of family and friends. In the case of forty or so of these friends, representing more than thirty families, that help took the form of filling in detailed questionnaires in which I asked them to share their ideas and experiences on all sorts of topics relating to Christian family life. I did this because I wanted the book to be broadly based, rooted in everyday life and practical – as well as biblical.

Everything that was sent to me has contributed to the book, in that it has enriched my thinking and given me much quotable material. Unfortunately, for reasons of space, I haven't been able to use as many contributions as I would have liked – but I appreciated all of them. Those that have been included, have pseudonyms attached to protect the privacy of the families concerned.

Since the book covers a vast topic, it was necessary to decide whether to concentrate on a few themes and cover them fairly fully, or range over more subjects in less detail. What I have tended to do is the latter, while trying to dwell as long as possible on the points which are raised most often by parents.

I am very conscious of all the omissions, not least of the grim problems which many families endure. Families in deep pain require a book on their own; I felt it would not be right to tuck them into one which is mainly about the ups and downs of normal family life. But I would want us all to be aware of and reach out to families torn apart by death or divorce or ground down by chronic illness, disease or any other severe difficulties.

Two other points: all Scriptural quotations are from the New International Version of the Bible; and I have referred to the child as 'him' throughout, simply and solely to avoid having to keep putting 'him/her'!

Finally, I would like to thank very warmly my family and every single person who has prayed, supported, shared or helped in any way.

I.

A gift and a task

As this book is mainly about children, it seems appropriate to begin it with the opening of a children's story.

Once upon a time, a farmer and his wife were looking round their orchard when they were astonished to see the king. Before they could speak, he strode across to them exclaiming, 'Just the people I wanted to see!' and then shook them warmly by the hand.

'We're honoured,' said the farmer. 'Would you like to come indoors?'

'No, thank you,' answered the king, much to the relief of the farmer's wife, for her house was not in the state she would have wished it to be for a royal visit. 'I find it very pleasant out here, so let's just walk and talk, if you don't mind.'

So they strolled around the orchard in the gathering twilight.

'I have been looking round my kingdom,' said the king, 'trying to find just the right people and places for growing some special trees for me until they are ready to be transplanted into the palace garden. And I have decided that you are two of the right people and that this orchard is one of the right places. Would you be willing to take and grow the seed of one of my special trees?'

'We would be delighted,' said the farmer, and his wife agreed.

'Thank you,' said the king, and he stopped walking and opened his hand to show them a tiny brown pip. The farmer took it, wrapped it carefully in his handkerchief and put it in his pocket. Then they went on walking while the king explained how to look after the plant so that it would grow into the right shape and size.

'Be careful to prepare the ground well,' he said, 'making sure that nothing will hinder the roots from growing deep into the soil so that the plant will be straight and strong. If you tend it well, in time it should grow into a sturdy tree bearing glossy leaves, cloudy blossoms and glowing golden fruit in their season. I hope you will enjoy its beauty, shade and fruitfulness.

'When I am ready, I will send my gardeners for the tree, and they will dig it up with great skill and transplant it to the place I have chosen for it in my palace garden, where it will bloom for ever.'

'Can you give us any idea of when that will be?' asked the farmer. There was no answer, and the king was nowhere to be seen. So the couple stopped walking and looked at one another, wonderingly.

'We must have been dreaming,' said the wife, but the farmer had taken his handkerchief out of his pocket and was opening it up, and they both saw that it held something tiny and brown . . .

As the pip of an apple contains the full potential for the tree, so the seed of a child contains the full potential of the adult. Whether a plant reaches its full potential depends on the quality of the seed, the tending it receives, the conditions and the soil.

So it is with the child. This book is about the soil, conditions and tending which parents and others need to provide if they want to promote deep roots, healthy growth and good fruit in their children's lives. But it's also about the child himself, and there the analogy breaks down, because the characteristics of a tree and a human being are so totally different!

Parents gazing into the wrinkled face of their newborn baby are usually filled with awe at the thought that this little life was created by them and belongs to them.

Christian parents can identify with these feelings, but there is an added dimension to our awe, because we know that the child is God's creation, too, and only given to us for the time being. We also know that God has given us the task of bringing him up well.

I believe that this involves giving him a *good*, *Christian* upbringing – with the emphasis on both words. Such an upbringing needs to be grounded in biblical principles and sound psychological insights, and these, rightly understood, will always be compatible since all facts are God's facts and all knowledge an insight into his ways of working.

Not all books on child care and development can be taken as 'gospel'. Those written by non-Christians, for instance, fail to take account of the child's spirit, however excellent they may be in other respects. So we have to read them critically, rejecting what does not tally with biblical truth. Even so, much good work has been done in this field and we can learn a great deal from it about the wise handling of our children and their physical, emotional and mental well-being, at each age and stage.

The Bible, on the other hand, while majoring on the spiritual aspect, *also* takes account of our bodies and minds (including will, intellect and emotions). So if we truly pattern our lives and our parenting on the principles it contains, and certainly if we also take the trouble to understand and apply the basics of child development, we will be able to avoid the two equal and opposite errors which I'd like to mention.

A super-spiritual upbringing

In some 'Christian' homes, parents fail to grasp the fact that they must take account of the *whole* child, and concentrate almost exclusively on the saving and growth of his soul. They therefore maintain a rather rarified atmosphere in the home – mixing with very few non-Christians and only like-minded Christians.[1]

Sooner or later, unless he becomes a monk, a child has to emerge from his hot-house to live and work in a college or office, shop or factory, where he is likely to stick out like a sore thumb. He may be able to discuss predestination, but has no small talk; he probably knows his Bible but is unsure of himself; he can cope with an hour of prayer, perhaps, but is unable to stand up to ordinary human interchange. It's possible, also, that temptations encountered for the first time, may hit him with sledgehammer force.

When people misunderstand, ignore or dislike him, he may comfort himself with the thought that he is suffering for Christ's sake and being 'salt' and 'light' in his world – but this may not be so. It could be his lop-sided personality and lack of social grace that are getting him dubbed as 'unreal' or even 'unbalanced' – not his Christian principles or witness at all.

Quite rightly he is not 'of' the world, but he's not really 'in' it either – let alone capable of overcoming it, by faith.

A worldly Christianised upbringing

At the opposite end of the spectrum are the parents whose lifestyle is practically indistinguishable from that of their nice, respectable non-Christian neighbours, apart from attendance at church and meetings. They offend no one and challenge no one, and their honest answer to Christ's question, 'What are you doing more than others?' (Matt. 5:47) would have to be, 'Not a lot.'

The children in such a home grow up in an atmosphere of Christianised worldliness and any faith they have is unlikely

1. For an extreme example of this, read Edmund Gosse, *Father and Son* (Penguin).

to stand up to what the world, the flesh and the devil will thrust at them. On the other hand, children from super-spiritual homes *may* manage to retain their Christian beliefs throughout their lives, but their impact on others is likely to be minimal since they will be regarded as misfits in a sense that they were never intended to be.

Striking a balance

We are not, I believe, supposed to live in Christian ghettoes, protecting our children as much as possible from ordinary secular life and ricocheting from one meeting to another so as to keep ourselves alert for the Lord's return. Nor are we meant to feel at home and comfortable in this world while keeping in with God and his people.

Instead, we are meant to be like Christ, who lived in the midst of the world's squalour and splendour, pain and joy, but was wonderfully, devastatingly different from those around him, in his behaviour, qualities and attitudes. He did not lead his followers to the Judean desert to live in caves, but through the streets and market-places of Galilee to mix with people of every sort, and teach and show them the ways of a different world, a spiritual and eternal one in which true greatness is demonstrated through service and sacrifice, and motivated by unselfish love. Ultimately, we want our children to be like Christ and therefore to bring them up in a way which will be conducive to their growth in grace and knowledge of him.

If our children do become disciples of Jesus, they will certainly face hardship if not actual persecution. So we must do all we can to help them develop into well-integrated people, with strong, well-thought-out convictions. Otherwise they will make pretty unsuccessful revolutionaries. And since the revolution they hope to achieve can only be brought about by loving means, they will need to have some rather special qualities and characteristics.

A tall order, indeed, and who's responsible for carrying it out?

'Fathers, do not exasperate your children; instead, bring them up in the training and instruction of the Lord.' (Eph. 6:4).

The short answer is that we, the parents, are primarily and ultimately responsible for our children's upbringing, but other people can play a vital part, too. Experts in various fields, as well as friends and relations, can contribute to their mental, emotional and physical development and health. And church leaders, youth workers, godparents, writers and all sorts of other Christians can contribute to their Christian education, through informal contacts, talks, houseparties and camps, books, cassettes and films.

With all this help, we might be able to equip our children to cope reasonably well with their three score years and ten, but we certainly wouldn't be able to fit them for heaven. For that we need the activity and aid of the Holy Spirit. Only he can regenerate our children and give them spiritual life and power; only he can give Christian parents the necessary love and wisdom, as we seek to being up our children for life in this world and the next.

A good Christian upbringing

I believe a truly Christian upbringing will also be a good one, and vice versa. Such an upbringing, briefly defined, is *one in which children are gradually taught and shown a true picture of life, and encouraged to start living it God's way.* The rest of the book expands that definition in the context of family life today.

2.

Building up a true picture of life

So what's this true picture of life that we want to build up?
It's the biblical picture of life with God (Father, Son and
Holy Spirit) as absolutely crucial and central. Far too many
Christians behave as though they believe that God retired on
the seventh day and is now merely keeping an eye on the
universe in a general way. Nothing could be further from
the biblical view of God. He watches the doe bear her fawn,
gives orders to the morning, and provides food for the
raven. He sees the fall of one sparrow and knows the number of hairs on our heads. If you have lost sight of that sort
of God, read Job chapters 38 to 41, Psalm 104 and 139,
Matthew 10:29,30 over and over again, until you believe
them.

Our God planned and created, sustains and directs in the
most minute detail, everything and everyone, and we all
function best when we fit into his design and purposes for
us. Our personalities, abilities, capacities, relationships, possessions and circumstances are under his control and we are
ultimately accountable to him for the way we use his gifts. He
has plans for all that he has created and can weave his perfect
pattern, using the raw material of ordinary people and
everyday life and experience. The universe is his oyster and
he is the pearl in it.

The trouble is, most people do not believe this. They live as
though God didn't exist, and follow their own devices. God

allows them to do this, even though the results are misery and chaos, while longing for them to turn to him, so that he can set them free to start living his way.

How can we play our part in helping our children to grasp such a picture and live such a life? Absolutely crucial here are teaching and training, example and prayer.

TEACHING

Teaching in the course of daily living at home

Fix these words of mine in your hearts and minds; tie them as symbols on your hands and bind them on your foreheads. Teach them to your children, talking about them when you sit at home and when you walk along the road, when you lie down and when you get up. (Deut. 11:18,19).

The verses in Deuteronomy draw a wonderful picture of informal teaching at home, through questions and answers and comments in the context of ordinary home life. Modern parents can apply it to their own home situations. At mealtimes, on walks, at bedtimes, in the bath, when dressing and undressing, while playing and working – the facts of God's presence, provision, interest, relevance and help can spill out of us quite naturally, provided we truly believe them. Through our spontaneous comments our children can begin to see that all things come from God and all are dependent on him. Their toys are made from things he created, and he's glad to see them play happily and generously with them. Their family and friends, and everything else they have, were lovingly planned by him for them.

Bedtime or morning prayers fit naturally into this God-centred day and provide brief opportunities for learning more, as well as responding in prayer, love and praise.

As well as informal teaching, in view of all the counter-culture that they will meet as they grow older, our children need to be given systematic biblical teaching, geared to their ages and stages.

It is crucial to make such teaching programmes appropriate. Throwing a bucketful of Christian truth over children and hoping that some of it will stick shows a lack of respect for the child and for his Creator, who planned that he should develop stage by stage.

At a Christian boarding school, I was taught at a very young age about dying to self – long before I really knew who I was or could apply this teaching without feeling destroyed by it. This probably contributed to a feeling of worthlessness which I had for years. When I at last threw that off, I also threw overboard the doctrine of self-denial and self-crucifixion, and continued to reject it even after I had reached an age and stage when it could have been both appropriate and enriching.

Given at the right time, all God's truths bring light, life and healing. But mature spiritual insights offered to children young in years and faith can cause hurt and confusion.

The local church, i.e. other Christians, can play a very big part in teaching our children 'the whole counsel of God', but parents need to be remain interested and involved, so that they can back up and supplement, if necessary. On pages 148, 154, 155 there are suggestions as to what truths might be taught at the various ages and stages.

TRAINING

Train a child in the way he should go, and when he is old he will not turn from it. (Prov. 22:6).

To talk about training or disciplining our children is not popular today. We are told that discipline is not necessary and that if children are given the right teaching and example, they will respond positively. I have to disagree with those who take this view – on both theological and realistic grounds.

To err is human

The idea that if children are loved, shown and taught what is right, they will do it, is very appealing. Unfortunately, the well-taught and much-loved children that I know do not fit into that idyllic picture. They test their parents over and over again by overstepping the lines which have been drawn. Knowing what is right, they either don't choose or can't manage to do it. In theological terms, we would say that children, like adults, are fallen human beings, naturally drawn to the evil or the second-rate, while having glimmerings of goodness, excellence and perfection within them.

To discipline is divine

The Lord disciplines those whom he loves, and he punishes everyone he accepts as a son. (Heb. 12:6).

I believe children need training or discipline. But the verse gives us a far better reason for including it in the upbringing of our children: God, the perfect pattern for parenting, disciplines his children. It also gives the lie to the common belief that discipline (and, indeed, punishment – an even more taboo word) is incompatible with love, since God disciplines and punishes *because he loves!*

Christian discipline

Not all forms of so-called discipline are right and beneficial: only those motivated by a love that wants the child's highest good and tempered by a wisdom that perceives what this is and how to bring it about.

As parents, we must be ruthlessly honest with ourselves about our motives. Do we discipline our children to impress our neighbours, or because we need to be obeyed or to have the best-behaved children in the road? If so, our manner of disciplining will almost certainly be at fault. If our sights are set on ourselves or our neighbours, we could very easily fail to consider and ride roughshod over our child's personality. Unwise or unloving discipline will not be conducive to achieving the purpose of all good training. This is that the person concerned will come to experience true freedom – that of doing what he ought rather than what he likes.

Discipline at home

Fathers, do not exasperate your children; instead, bring them up in the training and instruction of the Lord. (Eph. 6:4).

Have you ever heard parents say, 'We'll give him love at home and the school can knock a bit of discipline into him'? This isn't an uncommon attitude, springing from a defective understanding of children, discipline and love! Ideally, children should be loved and disciplined both at school and at home, but *certainly* at the latter – the place where he is known and loved best and will therefore be disciplined most appropriately. Serious blunders can occur when people try to discipline children they don't know at all well or don't like much.

Different forms of discipline

Discipline is by no means all negative, and this should be remembered more often (see page 70). We ought to do at least as much encouraging our children in righteousness as discouraging them from unrighteousness. But we do have to do the latter at times.

A very common way of trying to control our children is through what we say and how we say it, i.e. the tone of voice or the facial expression we use. So we can use words to scold, nag, warn, be angry, threaten; tease, mock, make unfavourable comparisons; or evoke guilt, shame, sadness or regret.

Which of those do you think are compatible with Christian love and wisdom?

Anger and shouting. Anger is *sometimes* right, or righteous, and to express it by shouting or, if you prefer the euphemism, 'raising one's voice', is human and natural. Also, occasional and moderate anger, in response to deliberately bad behaviour, does some good and little or no harm, provided that it is balanced by at least as much praise and affection. In other words, if you are a shouter, be a hugger and kisser too! Parents who are only emphatic in telling off their children, will quickly discourage or demoralise them.

Also, as Christian parents, we should be growing more self-controlled. If we are not, and if we are *often* and *very* angry, we run the risk of damaging our children emotionally if not physically. Nor are we commending the Prince of Peace who gave meekness, gentleness, humility and self-control such a high priority in his life and teaching (see Matt. 5).

Recognising the truth about ourselves and praying alone and with trusted friends about the problem can change things for the better quite dramatically. Sometimes skilled counselling is also needed.

So, parents with short fuses need to be at least as positive in showing love and encouragement as in showing anger, preferably more so, and we ought to be working at and praying for greater self-control.

Ridicule and belittling. Being sarcastic to a child or comparing him unfavourably with others and making him feel inferior, ridiculous or hopeless will be very unhelpful in the long term. These may deter him momentarily from a course of action, but they are unlikely to motivate him to do right. On the contrary, such methods, if applied often, will probably crush his self-esteem and spirit, and set his will like iron against the wishes of those who belittled him.

Teasing and irony. In the context of a relationship of love and trust, mild teasing and gentle irony can help a child to see himself as others see him and perhaps motivate him to change. Cruel teasing, however, and heavy-handed irony, motivated by malice, will wound, anger or crush him. So we must be very wary of using these means (see also page 60).

Sadness

We can try to influence our children's behaviour and attitudes by telling them and showing them how upset they have made us, but we need to think through the implications of doing this.

> I remember telling our young son off for some misdemeanour, and stressing that I was both *angry* and *sad*. A little later I came across him, sitting hunched up at the bottom of the stairs and asked him what he thought about it all. I shall never forget his reply: 'I mind about the *sad*, but not about the *cross*.'
>
> This showed me clearly, if I didn't already know it, whether my sadness or anger would motivate this particular child more effectively. But later I came to see that we have to be careful about using parental feelings, whether of anger or sadness, to correct our children's behaviour, since they may well equate 'right' with what makes Mum and Dad pleased, and 'wrong' with what makes them sad or angry. Since we are fallible human beings, this can be very misleading. Nor is it much help in the long run, since ultimately we want our children to do right *because it's right* – not because they will upset us if they don't. (Di)

Trying to arouse feelings of guilt and shame in a child as a way of causing him to change, is certainly effective with some children. But is it right? Tina shares her memories and thoughts on this:

> My mother tried to make us feel guilty much of the time. If we agreed with Father over some dispute, she would say, 'You're always taking *his* side, not *mine*!' If we'd had a row, which, sadly, was a frequent occurrence, she would sidle into the bedroom in the morning and say, 'Did you have a good night?' If the answer was, 'Yes,' she would say, 'I didn't – I had an *awful* night.' And with that, she would depart.
>
> I remember her sitting by me once and stroking my arm as she said softly, 'You know I love you very much.' Then there was a pause, after which she added, 'But then, of course, you don't care whether I do or not.'
>
> When my husband and I didn't visit as often as it was thought we should, she would say, 'You hardly ever come to see us. All I can say is – there must be something very, very wrong.'
>
> When my sister and I, in our late teens/early twenties wanted to move away from home and become independent like other people, she became furious and said lots of horrid things, including that we were being ungrateful for all that had been done for us. (Tina)

Trying to manipulate our children's behaviour for our own selfish ends is clearly going to produce very bitter fruit. Even if we succeed in getting them to do as we want, there will be resentment inside them, and this will probably lead to rebellion sooner or later.

Does this mean that we should *never* make our children feel ashamed of themselves? I don't believe it does. There are times when they can behave better than they do, and if they don't appear to be aware of the fact, we probably ought to make them aware of it. Perhaps we could say something like, 'That was wrong/unkind/selfish. You let yourself/us/some-one else down by behaving like that.' Personally, I would want to avoid remarks such as, 'You made Jesus sad by doing that,' because I feel it's 'using' the Lord to manipulate our children's feelings and behaviour. Certainly, it is part of our job to help shape their consciences, but using religion as a stick to beat them with doesn't seem to me to be fair or wise. Others may disagree.

Also, we must beware of overdoing things. In the delicate business of conscience-moulding, we need to be sensitive to the Holy Spirit and have a healthy understanding of sin, guilt and forgiveness, as well as a compassionate, unselfish and realistic appraisal of our children's temperaments and what one might reasonably expect at a given age/stage. Of course, we want our children to know right from wrong and to be aware of their sinfulness, but this is a very different thing from being riddled with guilt, and far too many children emerge from Christian families in this condition.

Threats and warnings

Less strong-willed children may be deterred, at least for a time, from a course of action by threats and warnings, but only if they know from experience that we mean what we say.

For strong-willed children, words, however threatening, will not be enough. Sooner or later we will have to take action.

Non-verbal methods of trying to control our children

It's extremely easy to overdo scoldings, and when this happens, our children simply switch off. They stop hearing what we are saying and repeat the offence, which brings on more scolding and creates a bad atmosphere which can linger on and on.

The value of action

We can't divorce words and action entirely, of course, since we have to tell our children what we will permit and what we won't, and what action we will take if they choose to disobey us. But having done that, we can, if the child defies us, take the action we have promised, calmly and promptly. Disciplining through action has many advantages:

- it's specific: a child knows exactly what to expect if he does not toe the line
- it proves to the child that the parents mean what they say and will back it up
- it teaches the child that his choices bring consequences – unpleasant ones, if he opts to disobey
- it deters the strong-willed child more effectively than words
- it's clean: justice is done and seen to be done – and all can then put the matter behind them and have a fresh start
- it also seems to me that God uses action as well as words when he is disciplining his children.

What action?

Endless discussion surrounds the issue of smacking children. Extremists at one end advocate it indiscriminately, and at the other, they label it as child abuse!

Parents must decide on the action they feel is appropriate to their child, whether this is smacking (and if so, with what), sending him to his room, taking a privilege away from him or setting him a task. And having decided, they must act confidently and from faith.

I don't think it would be misusing Scripture to substitute 'acts' and 'action' for 'eats' and 'eating' in the following verse. The 'everything' in the second part of the verse can equally well embrace both ideas. 'But the man who has doubts is condemned if he eats, because his eating is not from faith; and everything that does not come from faith is sin.' (Rom. 14:23).

Many of us have been brain-washed into feeling guilty about punishing our children in any way. So we either scold or threaten instead, while feeling deep inside us that this is neither right nor very effective; or we take action, but diffidently and apologetically, so making a botched job of it, rather like half-cleaning a room and making more mess than if one hadn't started at all.

I believe parents need to work out biblical perspectives on training, discipline and punishment, and then take action, calmly and confidently, when it's appropriate.

When is action appropriate?

Action should be appropriate both for the child and the 'crime'. A timid, amenable child may hardly ever need action to deter him from wrong; a robust rebel may need quite a bit of it!

As far as what to punish is concerned, I think James Dobson's guidelines are very helpful. We should take action for wrongdoing, such as wilful and defiant disobedience of our authority as parents-in-charge. We should *not* take action for mistakes and accidents caused by immaturity.

If anyone had told me that our family ground-rules would ever need to include, 'Thou shalt not roller skate from the dining-room to the kitchen while carrying a jug of tomato soup', I should never have believed them. But anyway, one day our daughter did just that. Presumably the skates were a new toy and she couldn't bear to part with them. The result was that she had an accident and tomato soup was flung all over walls, carpet and floor.

Looking back later, I realised that the scolding I gave her was in proportion to the mess she had made, which was considerable, and *not* in proportion to the 'crime', which was unintentional, and accidental. (Di)

It's very hard to draw distinctions in the heat of the moment, but perhaps we should try to stop and think when something happens: 'Is this just a childish accident, which I need to make light of, or is there an important life-principle here, which I ought to make a real issue of?'

Guiding principles

Parents must choose their own guiding principles when it comes to deciding what forms of punishment are good and right.

As far as we are concerned, only those which are consistent with love, self-control and respect for our children, are permissible. Therefore, withdrawing love from a child, ridiculing or belitting him or using any form of physical or verbal violence is embargoed. No matter how effectively these may control behaviour in the short term, they will prove ultimately counter-productive.

How much teaching and pressure?

On the whole matter of teaching and disciplining our children, we have to be very wary of over-selling and over-pressurising.

It's much better to tell a child a little and leave him eager for more, than laying it on too thick. With church, Sunday School, Christian camps, boarding school, etc. I had had enough. I therefore never talked about Christian things until I had grown up and left home for fear of getting yet more.

It's interesting that my husband who did not have a Christian upbringing and became a believer at University, puts a higher premium on Christian teaching than I do. Looking back on my upbringing, I can see that its value lay not so much in the *volume* of Christian teaching that was given, as in the Christian lives of my parents, and in our home life. They had a capacity for love and understanding and taught us to be considerate and help with household chores and, for all their mistakes, we had a lot of fun. It wasn't until I was an adult, however, that the Bible became exciting for me. (Lisa)

We know of four children all pressurised to go to church and conform to Mum and Dad's mould of faith. All rebelled. All drink too much and have really gone mad with freedom. All are damaged with psychological guilt. If Christianity is to work, it needs two things – love and liberty. (Dawn)

On the other hand, human nature being what it is and the pressures of the world being what they are, our influence for Christ has to be pretty positive to have any effect at all. (Without some form of pressure, how many children would go to school every day?)

A friend of ours knows two families, one in which the children were rather pressurised to conform and the other in which they were given a good deal of freedom in matters of faith. The result, to date, is that *both* sets of children are pagan, the first being rather anti-parent also.

So we need God's love and wisdom to help us steer a middle course between pressurising our children and not influencing them enough. And, while taking account of our children's wishes, we mustn't let them be the only deciding factor in any situation. Of course we want, and will do everything in our power to help our children to *enjoy* Sunday School and church. But it would be unrealistic to expect them to be ecstatic about going every single time. They and their teachers and church leaders have their off days and the devil is active!

So most of us feel that it's right to let it be understood that worshipping and learning about God and meeting other Christians are simply things that Christian families do. Usually, where the family identity is a happy one, children will accept this attitude – even if they aren't deliriously happy about it. Of course if children are really unhappy for some time, we need to look into the situation sympathetically.

As they grow older, we have to allow them more freedom. Sometimes it works wonders to say, 'You may go to a place of worship somewhere, but it doesn't have to be the same as ours.' Or there may come a time when we feel that the wisest and ultimately most productive thing to say is, 'We want you to go to church, but you are now free to go or not to go.' Every parent must judge situations as they find them, and in the light of their knowledge of the children concerned.

Parents who put too much pressure on their children may well need to trust God more for them.

Trusting the Holy Spirit

I am concerned about parents or guardians who try to do the work of the Holy Spirit for him. I think the Bible story, or Chronicles of Narnia, or Little Lions, or whatever, should be told or read as they are, without application, and that we should allow the Holy Spirit to reveal the truth to the child's mind afterwards, at the right time. Therefore I also would want to avoid such pointed remarks as, 'You need the Lord in your heart. Why not ask him today? This will be the most important decision of your life.' (Hazel)

EXAMPLE

Set an example . . . in life, in love, in faith and in purity. (1 Tim. 4:12).

These words were written to leaders of Christian fellowships, but they are just as applicable to parents, since we are God's appointed leaders in those little households of faith – Christian homes. And our pattern for parenting is God himself. In the Bible, we see God's perfect parenting of his people: his love which wants and expects the best from them; his patience in teaching and showing them the same truths over and over again; his provision for their needs; his justice which insists on truth and fair dealing; his respect for their freedom of choice; his understanding of their weakness and immaturity; and his willingness to forgive and forget and start all over again. What a model! But we must pattern ourselves on it, in God's strength, if we want our children to 'grow in the grace and knowledge of our Lord and Saviour Jesus Christ'. (2 Pet. 3:18).

The 'do as I say, not as I do' principle simply won't work. It's no use telling our children that people matter more than things, if our reaction to an accidentally broken vase, for instance, shows we are more concerned about the damaged object than we are about the shock, fear or upset feelings of the child responsible for it.

Again, urging our children to value spiritual things more highly than material ones will have little impact if we spend much of our time, money and energy on acquiring and maintaining possessions.

Similarly, if our real motivation in buying new things, moving house or changing jobs is to keep up with or even outstrip the Joneses, it is hypocritical to exhort our children to 'do all for the glory of God', and they will see it as such.

We cannot be perfect, but we must be real and honest.

If we say that Christians should be different from those around them and that Jesus changes lives, then we ought to be different, attractively, and changing – for the better.

There can surely be no greater stumbling block to a child's faith than seeing that his parents' behaviour does not tally with their words. Our children are very ready to forgive our imperfections, if we admit them – but not our phoneyness, if we don't.

Christian parents who also admit their sin and inadequacy to God can have the abundant help of the Holy Spirit. This means they do not have to rely on their own goodness, wisdom, love, power or any other quality (Gal. 5:22).

Example is important in matters of faith, too. It's not enough for us to pray with our children; they need to see that we pray and read our Bibles too. I prefer to have my quiet times very privately and used to find myself rising hastily from my knees if I was kneeling down, or opening my eyes if I was sitting, the moment the children came into the room. One day it occurred to me that it would be much better to continue with my praying or reading even if I was interrupted. So this is what I now do. I still aim for and prefer privacy, but I no longer pretend I wasn't praying or reading the Bible if a child enters – not because I'm unaware of or want to disregard Jesus's teaching in Matthew chapter 6 verses 5 to 7, but because I believe it's important for children to know that we don't just tell them to read the Bible and pray every day – we do it too. This also shows the children that people do not necessarily grow out of such practices.

PRAYER

Nothing can be more important than praying for our children. Many couples pray for their children daily, together or individually or both. Some pray over their sleeping children, asking God to protect them in body, mind and spirit, and perhaps laying hands lightly on their heads as they do so. I heard of one Christian writer who would pray for the child whose bed she was making. (Hazel)

I like this imaginative linking of prayer and loving action. I have found it helpful, too, to write out a prayer for each child, thanking God for his personality and gifts, trying to put into words what it is we want God to do in and for him, and mentioning any problems in his life and character. Using such read prayers can be very helpful at times, particularly when one is feeling tired or churned up. Naturally, as children grow, these prayers will have to be rewritten to take account of changes in personality and situations. Using actual Bible prayers for our children, e.g. Eph. 3:14–19, is another powerful possibility.

What to pray for

We will want to pray for the whole child, perhaps focusing on one aspect of his development one day, another aspect the next.

> On Mondays I pray for our children's spiritual growth, on Tuesdays concerning moral issues, on Wednesdays – family relationships, on Thursdays – schools and careers, and on Fridays – relationships outside the family, particularly the opposite sex and future partners. (Emma)

At really difficult times, husbands and wives can find great strength in occasionally sharing and praying with close friends, or their children's godparents or Sunday school teachers/youth leaders. It's amazing what can happen when a group of committed Christians focus determinedly, and with faith and praise, on God for a particular situation.

Pray against the enemy

Often we see 'weeds' in our children's lives and know, with a sinking heart, that we sowed the seeds by things we said or did. But at other times we have to exclaim, 'We did *not* sow these seeds. An enemy has done this!' The devil will do his utmost to destroy the good seed from springing up in our children's lives and we must pray against him.

How much time do we spend praying with our partners, for our children particularly? Perhaps Hazel and Lionel's experience will challenge us to fresh commitment in this area.

We had been married for some time before it occurred to us that what we needed was to set aside an evening for thinking things through before the Lord. This was to be something different from quick goodnight prayers, family devotions at breakfast, or other brief prayer times.

We decided to start the evening with simple fasting – and prayed that neither telephone nor callers would interrupt. Our plan was to pray through the various issues, each following the other in prayer, and focusing on one problem at a time, from the same angle or different ones.

That was eight or nine years ago. Throughout that time, whenever possible, and health permitting, we have kept to our plan. You see, God stepped in and ironed out our difficulties so wonderfully that we found we couldn't do without this three-way consultation again, even when there were no problems.

I don't think there could be a more wonderful way for husbands and wives to keep in tune and touch with each other. Our marriage has gained a quality so precious that it is almost etherial, through this simple practice.

An evening's timetable could work out like this (on occasions we have used mornings instead):

6 p.m.	No meal. Singing favourite hymns and choruses together. The act of singing together so beautifully opens up the way to the evening's adventure.
6.30 or 7 p.m.	Taking turns in reading the next chapter of a helpful book.

7.30 p.m.	Turning what has been read into prayer, including prayers of worship.
8 p.m.	Discussing the topics we want to pray through that evening.
8.15 p.m.	Intercessory prayer.
9.30–10 p.m.	A drink of water and bed, knowing we have helped to advance the Lord's kingdom, and having received fresh impetus for our own lives in the coming week.

Such prayer requires discipline, but what a help it must be in the struggle to bring up children in a largely pagan world, where the enemy is very active. And what a relief it is, particularly when they are being wayward and difficult, to put our offspring into God's loving hands, with a cry for help.

When the children are appalling and I can't stand them, I can say, 'Lord, your children are being awful and I can't cope with them. Please do something about them.' A good buck passed! (Joan)

Encouraging and helping our children to live life God's way

While we are building up a true picture of life with God at its centre and head, we should also be encouraging our children to respond to what they learn by giving God his rightful place and facing life confidently, courageously, realistically and idealistically, lovingly, discerningly and responsibly. If they and we do that, in ways which I shall discuss in the following chapters, we will be making the most of this life as well as getting ready for the next. Not that we won't have opposition or suffering: Jesus had both, and warned us to beware if all men spoke well of us (Luke 6:26). But he also, generally speaking, found favour with man as well as favour with God; therefore we, who are growing by God's grace more like Jesus, can do likewise.

35

3.

Giving God his rightful place

We have talked about teaching, training, example and prayer but 'experience is the best teacher' and so we need to provide opportunities for our children to respond to what they learn from us and, indeed, to participate actively in the learning process. After all, the object of teaching a child that God is crucial and central to all life, is so that he will make him crucial and central in *his* life.

If we want to live God's way, our number one priority is to give God his rightful place. This involves, first of all, trust and obedience. Gratitude towards God, and friendship with him, are also very important. These are aspects of keeping the first commandment: 'Love the Lord your God with all your heart and with all your soul and with all your mind and with all your strength.' (Mark 12:30).

TRUST

Trusting Jesus as Saviour and obeying him as Lord

Trust in the Lord with all your heart. (Prov. 3:5).
If you confess with your mouth, 'Jesus is Lord,' and believe in your heart that God raised him from the dead, you will be saved. (Rom. 10:9).

What have trusting and obeying Jesus got to do with giving God his rightful place? They have *everything* to do with it, because God cannot be what he wants to be to us – friend, guide, helper – unless we come to him through Christ. There is no other way he can forgive us and accept us into his presence (John 1:12; 14:6). We need to believe this, and teach this truth to our children.

Teaching our children to trust

Our children must learn to trust a human being or they will not be able to understand what trusting God means, let alone do it. There are many people who cannot really trust God because their early experiences of people taught them to be wary and tense. Anxious parents often produce anxious children. So do unreliable ones.

Very soon our baby will know whether he can trust us or not, though it will be a long time before he actually understands this. If we learn to interpret his movements, sounds and facial expressions and meet his needs promptly, calmly and lovingly, we are laying good foundations for building a personality capable of trusting others. The same thing applies when we unfailingly give our toddler the reward or punishment we promised him.

Many authority figures in our children's world are not trustworthy. How devastating it must be for a child to discover that even his parents' word is not definitely their bond if, having vowed before God and the Church to be faithful to death, they opt out when the going becomes hard.

Christian parents are human and cannot be a hundred per cent dependable all the time, but with God's help, we can be those on whom our children feel they can rely and are happy to do so. This is likely to make them receptive to teaching about God's utter trustworthiness, and encourage them to trust their whole lives to him.

Jesus welcomed and blessed young children and told the near by adults: 'Unless you change and become like little child ren, you will never enter the kingdom of heaven.' (Matt. 18:3)

If children are wisely taught and influenced through prayer and example, they can respond very early with real faith and genuine commitment, and be truly born again by the Holy Spirit.

At ten years of age, while cycling to church one day, one of our sons said that he thought he would like to give his life to the Lord. We discussed it and left it for him to think through. The talk in the service was 'just right' and while we were on our way home he said, 'I've done what I said.' We quietly accepted it and gave him a postcard of Jesus the Light of the World, to keep in his Bible as a reminder.

Our second son, aged eight, went to a meeting and stayed behind afterwards. He didn't tell us this, but his brother and one of the leaders there let us know about it. Our son is quiet and reserved, but he dropped a few hints in his prayers, and then, two days later, came into the kitchen and said, 'Haven't you noticed anything? I think since I've become a Christian, I've been helped to get on better with my little sister and not annoy her.' (Hugh)

Whether or not children make a definite, specific commitment like the ones described above, I personally believe it's right, in the context of Christian family life and a home based on Christian principles, to treat them as fellow-believers in and disciples of the Lord Jesus.

'I am convinced that we must look upon *all children* as being included in the great atoning sacrifice of Calvary. They belong to Jesus Christ and to God until such time as they may deliberately refuse him.'[1] I appreciate that not everyone would agree with this view, but this is not the place to enter

1. John Inchley, *All About Children* (Coverdale).

into all the pros and cons of the debate about whether children are 'in' until they reach the variable and hard-to-define age of accountability and opt 'out', or vice versa. But parents who take Inchley's view are likely to have a more relaxed and less pressurised approach to their children's Christian education. They tend to see themselves as co-operating with the Holy Spirit, already at work, they believe, in the child, instead of focusing on promoting an act of commitment from him.

True, God has no grandchildren, but we become his children in different ways, although only through Jesus and by the activity of the Holy Spirit. Some children can look back on a moment of decision which was a major turning point. But others may have responded naturally and spontaneously to all that they were taught in the home from their earliest years, and be genuine disciples, growing in faith, without being able to say exactly when they were 'converted'. The important point is whether or not the direction of one's whole life is Godward, through faith in Christ and obedience to his Spirit. An act of commitment, or any number of acts of commitment, are valuable in so far as they contribute to the same spiritual end.

Whatever our views may be about children and the Kingdom, we would probably all agree that a child's spontaneous responses and unquestioning trust are lessons to older people. We should, I think, accept our young as parts of the Body of Christ – today's Church – and be prepared to welcome their contribution as well as to minister to them.

The maturing of faith

Faith and trust need food and exercise if they are to grow. God's word, worship and all other forms of prayer and praise, and God's people are vital here.

As with other sorts of growth, the growth of faith may not be smooth, but a series of ups and downs. A very up-and-down patch is likely to occur during older adolescence, when the young person may test his faith against alternative lifestyles and religions before deciding whether to reject it or make it his own in a more mature, adult way than before.

It would be easy for parents to panic at such times. Staying calm, allowing doubts to be voiced, answering questions and praying very hard that our young people will sort themselves out before they have to make big decisions such as what job to do or who to marry, are more helpful attitudes. At the same time, we can keep trusting God, who can overrule even bad mistakes and weave them eventually into his good pattern for the lives of those who made them (perhaps in a period of backsliding).

OBEDIENCE

Teaching our children to obey

Children, obey your parents in the Lord, for this is right. (Eph. 6:1).

> The object of bringing up children is so that they will grow into adults who are obedient to God. Such obedience will involve saying 'No' both to themselves and to others, and may be very costly. Therefore children from an early age need to learn the importance of obedience and to accept discipline. (Joan)

The Bible pattern for authority in the home is that parents should obey God and children should obey parents, and so learn to obey God.

Obedience and young children

When our children are small, we will do as much distracting as we can when they want to unplug the television or hit a playmate over the head with a wooden block. But babies are not distractable for ever. They grow into determined toddlers. So we soon find ourselves having to say some very firm 'No's', following this up with action if necessary. Some toddlers and pre-school children will react to not getting their own way by throwing temper tantrums. However violent the scene, and wherever it takes place, we must never, never let them have what they want or give in, *because* it's the easiest way out of the situation. Whatever we feel like inside, we must remain outwardly calm and make it perfectly clear that, while we quite understand how strongly they feel, this way of showing it is always unprofitable (see also page 132).

As our children grow older, we will be asking for their co-operation in more and more ways. Having told them to put away their toys, wash their hands, go to bed, put on their coats – what then? Do we expect instant obedience or allow a little leeway?

> We've always given our children the one-two-three option. It allows two counts of defiance before final capitulation, and also cools the temper reaction of parents. (Lesley)

> Stop nagging and expect your child to obey you the first time – and whatever you threaten, carry out, no matter how inconvenient it may be. (Nita)

Punishing disobedience in young children

Lesley and Nita have different approaches – and that's to be expected, since parents and children vary so much. More importantly, both would be agreed about the outcome. The child is to do as the parent wishes, or else . . . ! What happens when the parents *don't* mean what they say is illustrated in the story below:

I once invited a hyperactive child and his mother to tea. As soon as they arrived, the boy, Bill, began to run wildly all over the house and garden. I didn't mind too much: I knew what he was like. But his mother said, 'If you walk all over the flowerbed again, I'll take you straight home without any tea.'

'Will you really?' I thought. 'And just when I've baked a special cake for the occasion.' But Bill's mother had no intention of taking him home and Bill knew it. He walked all over the flowerbeds several more times. He'd got his mum exactly where he wanted her, and she felt embarrassed by her obvious defeat. I've fallen into the same trap myself many times. (Denise)

Keith's experience was similar up to the first warning – but how different things were from that point onward!

I took Judy out to tea when my wife Harriet was ill, and she proceeded, quite purposely, to play me up. I warned her, but she didn't stop, so I excluded her from the room. It was the first time I had ever done this, and boy! – did it hurt!

The sequel was when we were going home. Judy, in the push-chair, just looked up into my eyes and said, 'Daddy, I love you!' Divine vindication, that!

Keith acted promptly and this is vital in punishing young children. Deferred punishments lose their point. Instant smacking, scolding or removal from an enjoyable situation can be very effective.

We do smack (bottoms) when the occasion calls, begs and pleads for it, but we try to explain clearly why we are going to smack, so that it's not lashing out in anger. Charles especially, if warned that a course of action would merit punishment, will sometimes decide that it's worth it and, after doing the thing, come for the smack. (Rebecca)

Many parents smack with their hands, but James Dobson's point is worth considering here. He believes the hand should always be seen as an object of love, and therefore advocates using some other suitable object.

After the punishment, a cuddle is in order (in no way to be seen as an apology for punishment rightly administered) so that harmony can be restored and the matter forgotten.

Putting things right

Sometimes part or even all of a child's punishment will involve reparation.

> We had been out to tea with friends and one of our children had taken a fancy to a small toy which she had secreted about her person. I was not aware of anything untoward until we arrived home and the child began to sidle up-stairs. On being asked what she was hiding, she produced the toy. We immediately returned to the friend's house to give it back. The child knew she had done wrong and was fearful of the reception we would get, but it was a lesson which had to be learnt. The friend was predictably under-standing. I wish she had just taken the toy back, but she said that if the child liked it so much, she must keep it. The toy was brought home but totally rejected.
>
> We had one further incident after this. The same child arrived home from a birthday party with her knickers fairly bulging with goodies. Temptation had been too much for her when she had seen the abundance of gifts round the birthday child. The same procedure as before was adopted. This time the lesson went home. (Lucy)

Obedience and older children

As our children grow older, there will be all sorts of new issues about which we will need to make decisions. Before our children grow into adolescents, it would be wise for us to be very clear as to what we will and will not permit, with well-thought-out reasons. This would apply to parties, drinks, drugs, pre-marital sex, abortion, films, magazines, television and music. Our children may have no intention of taking drugs or being promiscuous, but they will certainly want to see whether we have thought these things through properly. If they respect us and our opinions, we have a very good basis for discipline.

I have a feeling that some of us are so worried about alienating our young people by laying down the rules we believe in, that we fail to give the firm lead that is needed and sometimes even wanted. Parents who tolerate anything and everything are really telling their children that their standards aren't important, or that they don't care enough to take strong action and face the possible scenes.

My husband and I very reluctantly decided not to allow our son to go to a particular function, but when we told him so, instead of the expected protest, I was given a beaming smile and the words: 'Thanks, Mum!' I realised then that though he hadn't been mature enough to turn the invitation down in his own right, he *wanted* to do so, and we had made this possible and easy for him.

Since then, when telling our children that we aren't going to allow them to do something, we have sometimes added, 'And you can blame it on us, if you like.' I feel this is a help, although eventually we want them to take responsibility for themselves. (Di)

At times, our children will definitely *not* want us to take a firm line, but we may feel we simply have to do so, no matter how unpopular it makes us. For instance, children may want to have a party at home, and would prefer their parents to be out for the evening. But Mum and Dad may feel – quite rightly, I think – that it's better for them to be around, however inconspicuously, to exert a sobering influence, or intervene if necessary. We know of parents who have left their houses only to return to face horrifying messes or even breakages. Their own children had been so sure they could handle things, but they had been wrong. Fortunately, good can come out of situations like this, in that children can be more realistic about themselves and others, and parents can see where to draw the line in future.

Punishing disobedience in older children

> The daughter of a friend of ours wanted her ears pierced 'like everyone else in my year at school'. The parents talked about it but did not give their permission. The following Saturday the daughter came home with her ears pierced – she and her friend having done it to each other with blocks of ice and darning needles. The parents were horrified and angry, sent the studs back to the friend, and closed the matter until such time as their daughter reaches the age of sixteen. The daughter is exceedingly angry about all this. (Mary)

I wonder how you react to that story. What would anger and grieve me most is not the ear-piercing, but the deliberate flouting of parental wishes. The principle that parents should be in charge still applies when the children are adolescents. Hopefully, there will be fewer rules and prohibitions at this stage and these could be talked over with the young people, and their views listened to. The rules should nonetheless be adhered to. If they are not, then we will have to take action.

But what sort of action is appropriate to these age groups?

Where there is deliberate defying of reasonable parental authority, we feel that pocket money reduction is fair enough for fifteen-year-olds. Sometimes if our time limits are broken, for instance, we ask the young person to give back the time in service to the family; e.g. someone who's an hour late should do an hour's gardening or window cleaning. Provided that we stated our time-rule clearly and the children were aware of this, we usually received their co-operation. (Mary)

Appropriate discipline would be honesty and effective sanctions, e.g. money, food, liberty. (Derek)

Know your child and punish appropriately, e.g. stop food for the greedy, clothes for the vain, money for the spend-thrift, etc. (Joan)

In the context of a loving home, punishments and deterrents such as having to do a task or miss an enjoyed privilege are effective in many cases. But for some children, more desperate measures may be needed, as Vicky shares.

In our family, two of our children are obliging and co-operative. The third has objected to discipline all her life and disrupted the peace without fail by making constant scenes and battling over any and every issue. She seems to thrive on verbal and physical fighting. Regrettably we haven't been able to provide her with the discipline or authority she has needed. Strangely enough, she also depends on me for decisions and advice.

In the end, after much heart-searching, we sent her to boarding school, where we hoped she would gain independence and receive authoritative discipline. This has improved things at home and seems to be having a good effect on our daughter.

Why the emphasis on obedience to parents?

We want our children to obey us because:
● God has said that this is right (Eph. 6:1)
● it adds to their security: 'A child who assaults the loving

authority of his parents is greatly reassured when their leadership holds firm and confident.'[2]
- with God's help, we should be the best judges of what's good for them
- it should prepare them for life when they will have to obey the laws of the land (Rom. 13:1) and, if they are to reap spiritual blessings, the laws of God (Deut. 28:2).

Obedience to all authority figures

As was mentioned, we have to teach our children to obey us as part of training them to obey all in authority. This is God's plan for both children and adults.

The trouble is, our children are likely to encounter authority figures who are hard or uncaring, selfish or disloyal, impure or profane, or unable to give the lead and exert the control they should. It can be at secondary school, or even earlier, that they come across people who show some of those characteristics.

What are we, as parents, to do when our children meet authority figures who are unworthy of their position? Should we allow them to be critical, or clamp down firmly on all 'disloyal' comments?

On balance, it seems right to let them express their feelings, but we should discourage them from exaggerating and from being really rude to and about their teachers. In an atmosphere of reasoned discussion we can ask for their comments and perhaps point out, from our wider experience of life, why someone said or did something, and also suggest ways of responding that might improve the situation. Or we may have to admit that we don't understand and don't agree with what is happening, while stressing that it's right for children to behave respectfully – even if they don't feel the person concerned is worthy of respect – because:

2. James Dobson, *Discipline While You Can* (Kingsway).

- this is likely to improve the situation, while being cheeky and disobedient is likely to make it worse
- God commands us to submit to those in authority (he put them there and could remove them from their position if he wanted to, and the fact that he doesn't must mean that he's allowing the situation to continue for some good, if inscrutable, reason).

Obedience to God

We have to teach our children that obedience to God takes priority over every other form of obedience (Acts 5:29) and that, in practice, it means living up to his standards generally and discovering and fitting in with his specific plans for us as individuals. So we need to start helping our children to listen to God as he speaks through Scripture, prayer, conscience, circumstances and other Christians. When it comes to choosing a career, or making any other decision, they can be encouraged to seek God's guidance.

I think we can assure them that although God's will won't always be exactly what they want, it won't necessarily be the opposite either. Jesus said his yoke was 'easy' and 'light' (Matt. 11:30), and I take this to mean that he gives us concerns and work which are suitable and fitting to us as individuals.

WORSHIP

Come, let us bow down in worship, let us kneel before the Lord our Maker. (Ps. 95:6).
Worship the Lord your God, and serve him only. (Matt. 4:10).

Worshipping and enjoying God is another, very vital, aspect of giving him his rightful place. If we can enable our children to worship him whole-heartedly and joyfully, we will be helping them towards the chief end of their creation as human beings. Being 'lost in wonder, love and praise', caught up in the enjoyment of God for who he is, is an experience beyond any other known to humans. And the Bible makes it clear that children can know something of this blessing and that God values their praise. (Ps. 8:2).

Worship at home

From the earliest days, this can take place at regular prayer-and-story times, as well as throughout the day in spontaneous expressions of praise and love to God. A small child can very soon and very naturally lift his being towards God saying, in one way or another, 'I'm so glad you're here. I love you. How good you are!' And that, surely, expresses the essence of worship.

Individual prayer-times

We want our child to grow into a personal relationship with God, but for some years we will need to set the pattern for individual prayer-times and help him to make the best use of them. A regular time, and perhaps a regular place, are good. First thing in the morning and last thing at night are popular but there's nothing sacred about either. The main thing is that parents and children should feel relaxed, and that the proceedings should be short and enjoyed by all. Some element of worship should always be present when we turn to God and we should try to communicate and encourage this.

As the children grow older, they can be given notes with suggestions of short Bible passages to read and comments on them. We should go on sharing these times as long as our children need or want us to. Then, when they want to be on their own, we should keep encouraging, but not nagging, and praying that this practice will develop into a true walk with God.

Reading the Bible

The Bible is not an easy book to understand, even in modern translations, so we do need to introduce its contents wisely and little by little, doing our best to help children see Bible reading as a way of discovering God's secrets and his messages to us.

Family prayers

Some families do manage family prayers, at least for a time, and find it a great strength. Again, worship can be encouraged at these times. Here are some ideas as to what family prayers might include, at different times:

- a story or passage from the Bible
- some singing, preferably Scripture in song
- a verse of the week which the family learns together
- a cassette to be enjoyed and discussed
- mini-dramas or mimes
- prayer and praise
- impromptu picture-drawing or model-making.

When our son was little, we used to have Bible story-telling time when Dad would draw stick figures to illustrate what he was saying as he went along – all in a special notebook which I've kept for fifteen years because it's so precious. (Hazel)

Family prayers can have great value so long as everyone enjoys them. Otherwise, it's best to drop them and get the family together on an occasional basis – when important family decisions have to be taken, for instance.

Worship in church

As well as worshipping God at home, our children need to experience worship in church with other Christians – both in

Junior Church or Sunday school and at all-age services. It's very natural for young children to express their feelings through their bodies, so worship for them may well mean singing, clapping, tapping, dancing, playing on a musical or percussion instrument, and generally expressing exuberant joy in such ways.

Jewish celebrations must have been ideal for young children, with all their colour, movement, activity, ritual, music, recitation, special food and excitement. How children must have enjoyed the processions, and activities such as building and living in booths! On these occasions, they were not told to 'sit still and shut up', but encouraged to ask questions and participate. Would that services in churches today could have more of the flavour of these Jewish celebrations!

As our children grow older, we need to be sensitive to their means of communication and to make it possible for them to worship in a style and idiom which mean something to them.

Other Christians

As well as worshipping with other Christians, we can have fun with them. We and our children need – and God planned that we should have – deep, supportive friendships with other Christians, so that we can help one another to worship, witness, work and live for him.

Church houseparties, picnic lunches and games sessions on Sundays after church in the summer, harvest suppers, barn dances, games/musical/literary/home-made-entertainment evenings – these are some of the ways in which Christians can get to know each other and give and receive of one another's talents, at all age levels.

Making Sunday special

We kept a Sunday box which appeared only on the first day of the week. The books in it did not necessarily have to be religious but they were different and only for Sundays, as were the puzzles, games and colouring pens. In my childhood, Sundays were associated with five meetings per day and feelings of boredom. (Hazel)

We want Sunday to be a day with a difference, but we need to think out what that difference should be. To put too much emphasis on its being a day for God could be unhelpful, since every day is a day for God and the implication might otherwise be that it's only necessary to behave like citizens of heaven on the first day of the week!

In the Bible, the emphasis seems to be on having a day free from normal work routines and free for rest, change and, above all, spiritual refreshment and refocusing (Gen. 2:2,3; Isa. 58:13; Mark 2:27).

So Sunday should be different in its choice of priorities – not in kind. We don't honour God more on Sundays than we do on other days; we honour him in different ways. Special meals, family outings and games can help to make Sunday a happy day for everyone.

GRATITUDE

Give thanks in all circumstances. (1 Thess. 5:18).
Every good and perfect gift is from above, coming down from the Father. (Jas. 1:17).

An appreciative, grateful attitude goes right against the prevailing idea that everyone is entitled, for some reason that's not clear to me, to be safe, happy, fulfilled, well-housed, well-fed, well-clothed and probably well-heeled too! These things are regarded as rights to be snatched and fought for. People feel cheated and resentful if they don't have them.

The Christian view is that we have a right to *nothing*, and that all we have and are spring from God's love and generosity. If we truly believe this, and our whole attitude shows it, our children will catch the same outlook. An attitude of gratitude is infectious – as is an attitude of discontent! Children can be infected very early.

Saying grace before meals is good, provided it doesn't become mechanical and dull.[3] Nor should food be the *only* thing we give thanks for during the day. Happy times when we have enjoyed particular people, places or things can lead to spontaneous prayers such as: 'We've had such a good time on this walk/in this room/with this toy/friend. Thank you.' Presents, money and the things it buys, holidays, the seasons, plants, wildlife, pets, parties, hobbies, things we're good at are other blessings which our children can learn to appreciate and be grateful for.

There are plenty of good books, for young children particularly (e.g. *Thank You for a Loaf of Bread/Pair of Jeans*, Lion Publishing), which help to underline the truth that God is the behind-it-all giver and provider.

Thanksgiving should always be included in prayer-times at home and at church and Sunday school. It would be very helpful if older Christians could exude grateful, positive attitudes when meeting and talking informally. Sadly, many – like the Israelites of old – grumble about their church leaders, or else about the services or their fellow-Christians. This must be counter-productive, as is pulling the Sunday sermon to shreds at Sunday lunch in our children's hearing.

Grateful attitudes are not hard to have when everything is going well. It is when difficulties occur that the test really comes. If we still go on praising God when life is tough and trust him to bring good out of the problems, this will demonstrate a deep spiritual principle of blessing and victory to our children which will stand them in good stead as they mature.

3. For new ideas, try Carolyn Martin, *A Book of Graces* (Hodder & Stoughton).

FRIENDSHIP WITH GOD

Do not be anxious about anything, but in everything, by prayer and petition, with thanksgiving, present your requests to God. (Phil. 4:6).

The first way of encouraging our children to share all their news with God is by being willing to listen to all they want to tell us.

The other evening my son started to talk about a certain tennis star and I showed a sudden weariness and impatience which hurt him and he said, 'I'm trying to talk to you, and you sigh and tell me to go to bed.' I apologised and we made it up. Next morning as I was leaving for school, I said, 'You can talk to me about anything, including X (naming the star).' He grinned and I knew all was well. I realise how easy it is to brush off as trivial something that our child might feel is important. Whatever is important to him, shouldn't be trivial to us. (Di)

As well as learning to be good listeners, we can encourage our children to bring all their news, needs and wishes to God, and so to start developing a relationship of friendship with him. The quality of that friendship will owe much to the quality of their human friendships (see page 59ff.).

4.

Facing life confidently

For God did not give us a spirit of timidity, but a spirit of power, of love and of self-discipline. (2 Tim. 1:7).

Living life God's way involves giving him his rightful place first and foremost, but I believe he also wants us to face life confidently. Therefore we must help our children to grow into people who do face life with this attitude. This does *not* mean that all Christian parents should be producing bubbly extroverts. It *does* mean that, whether our children are straightforward and outgoing or complex and shy by nature, they will all have the necessary inner confidence to cope positively with life. This quality of confidence comes from *feeling safe, important and worthwhile; having a realistic and positive view of oneself; facing and overcoming difficulties;* and *learning to be both stable and flexible.*

There is no question of producing cocky egotists, blind to their own faults; our aim will be rather to play our part in promoting the development of people who know their true worth and significance. As Christian parents we can give this kind of assurance on two levels: the human and the divine. Because I believe this quality of confidence is so important in enabling our children to face 'the heart-ache and the thousand natural shocks that flesh is heir to', as well as the added hardships which result from being *in* but not *of* this world, I want to suggest thirteen 'roots' from which it might grow, and the part we can play (see also the diagram on page 156). The first 'root' is acceptance.

55

ACCEPTANCE

Accepting them as they are

It sounds obvious, but many parents do not really accept their children as they are – as far as basic personality, gifts and appearance are concerned. It's quite possible to accept in theory that our children are gifts from God (Ps. 127:3) while in practice deciding what our gift is going to look like and what it will be for – even before we get it properly unwrapped let alone take a good look at it. Clearly it would be ridiculous to decide to put Aunt Edna's present on the piano before taking the wrapping paper off, since it might prove to be a hammer instead of the vase we were hoping for or expecting. Isn't it equally ridiculous, as well as unloving and unwise, to have a child's whole career virtually mapped out in our minds before we have had time to get to know him, and then accept what we know?

Maybe we were hoping for a blue-eyed blond with agile limbs and a quicksilver brain. But what God gave us was a stocky brunette with two left feet and slow thought processes. So we may have to drop all ambitions about producing a professional sportsman or a university don, and set about making our child feel loved and accepted as he is.

One way of helping ourselves and our children in this area of acceptance is to avoid comparisons.

Comparisons are odious

It's very natural for parents to compare their babies and toddlers with those of friends, relatives or neighbours. And it can be a way of checking that our children are making normal progress. But generally speaking, comparison-making is unproductive.

Particularly when their children are small, mothers are prone to worry unnecessarily about relatively unimportant things. I was helped in this area by a friend who said, 'When you're worried about something to do with your child's progress or lack of it, ask yourself, "Will this be a problem when he's twenty-one?" If the answer's "No," then relax and let things take their course.' Following this advice, I developed a better sense of proportion in relation to walking, talking, eating and potty-training – since I was sure that my children would not have problems in any of these areas by the time they were twenty-one!

I think many of us waste far too much time on things that will normally sort themselves out – probably better and more quickly the less we fuss about them – and far too little on really important matters, such as whether our children are loving, sharing and generally relating well to people, and developing positive attitudes to life.

Thinking of the older child, I would like to put academic qualifications in the category of things we waste far too much time on, while recognising that these things do matter. But within the context of Christian family life and our goals for our children, I would wish to de-emphasise such qualifications, and pray that in time our young people will see all these things in their proper perspective. And I believe that will mean rating creative and practical gifts as highly as academic ones.

Comparisons can increase our pain

I think Walter's comments illustrate this more clearly than any words of mine could:

Apart from Cindy's obviously misshapen nose, her faulty hearing and vision have slowed her down considerably in her responses and perceptions. Without consciously comparing her with others, I am even more aware of her handicaps when observing other children's responses in these areas.

Also, there is her brother, who walked at eleven months (she, at twenty-six), was potty-trained at two (she has made no progress at three), and talked at the same age (she has no clear vocabulary) . . .

Comparisons can lead to superior attitudes and disappointed feelings

If our child compares unfavourably with others and we are disappointed, this can affect and damage his self-esteem enormously; if favourably, and we feel proud, this can make him feel smug or self-sufficient – both attitudes being displeasing to God.

Different areas of acceptance

It's clear that acceptance of our child has to be applied three-dimensionally.

We have to accept his age and stage for one thing. When I was running a pre-school playgroup, I once had a mother coming to see me because she was very worried about the 'naughty' behaviour of her three-year-old. He was, she said, always on the go, made a lot of mess, kept touching things, hated sitting still . . . and so on. I told her that her son wasn't really naughty; he was a classic three-year-old, and if he had been passive, incurious and docile, she really would have had cause for concern! (See pages 149–153.)

Then, we have to accept him as himself, with his own unique variations on the qualities and characteristics of others at a similar age and stage. This level of acceptance is absolutely crucial. We must show our child in as many ways as possible that: '*Most of all I love you 'cos you're you!*'

Also, we have to accept him as human – and that means sinful and fallible, just like us. Accepting our children's imperfections doesn't, of course, mean doing nothing to help them change. We are all imperfect, and if our children see us accepting our sinfulness while asking God's and other people's forgiveness, and trying hard – with God's help – to do better in future, they will be more likely to face up to their own faults and handle them positively. During the teenage years particularly, our children can become devastatingly aware of the good and evil within them, and we can help a great deal by our example, by Christian teaching, and by accepting them 'warts and all', as God does, while giving them hope that they can change where they should.

God's acceptance

On the basis of our acceptance, we can teach that God accepts more perfectly at all those levels and, while accepting us as we are for the time being, sees us as we could and should be and can start on the job of making us like that as soon as we let him.

CLOSE RELATIONSHIPS

The quality of the relationship between husband and wife is crucial here. If it's deep and close and shows in the way we respond to one another, it will have an effect on everyone else in the home.

Family relationships

With the birth of a baby, a couple becomes a family and their love expands to include the new arrival. His need for at least one person to depend on utterly is overwhelming. If his mother meets his needs and gives her love freely, she will receive the beginnings of her baby's adoring love in return. She will normally be giving more of her time and energy to the baby, but the earlier his father can become a known and loved figure in his world, the better for both of them.

Playing with the baby is exactly the right relaxant after a busy, responsible day at work! However, many men lack the confidence to handle small children happily. Their wives need to be aware of this and encourage them to shed their dignity along with their working clothes and become adept at bathing and playing games with their small sons or daughters.

It is through contacts with his parents first, and then with other relatives and friends, who make him feel safe, satisfied and happy, that a baby starts learning to love.

Weathering conflicts

Good relationships once formed do not stay that way for ever. There are bound to be strains and conflicts. If these are weathered well, the relationships are strengthened, and much is learnt.

Many of the verbal and physical tussles between brothers and sisters are a form of play and a useful way of letting off steam and learning about oneself and others. So parents may only have to keep a watchful eye on things and be tolerant of their young at play.

Teasing

One of our children, Pat, has a problem with reading, writing and spelling. So any references to her as 'thick' are strongly discouraged, but we, as family, have found one way of maximising on her weakness with words. We have learnt to laugh, together, at her 'malapropisms', e.g. her reference to a 'cycling sufficiency' test or to a friend who had her 'independence' out, so that they have given her a bit of extra kudos rather than a greater sense of failure. When we fall about at some new howler, she gives a mock sigh and says, 'I suppose that's another "Pat"ism,' and then laughs with the rest of us. (Di)

This kind of teasing might not work in a different situation. In fact, any kind of teasing has to be watched, as it can so easily lapse into cruelty and malice (see page 23). Each family will have to make its own rules so that teasing may be enjoyed without real hurt resulting. For instance, it might be necessary for parents to stop all references within the family to a fat child as 'Pud', or to a large-eared one as 'Dumbo', no matter what happens in the outside world.

What should we do when fights are *not* playful or laughter kind? In some situations we will need to act as arbiter and peacemaker, but ultimately we want our children to be able to cope for themselves. This will involve encouraging them to distinguish between harmless and harmful verbal or physical fights and tussles. We could ask, for instance, 'Why do you think things went wrong this time? How can you avoid the same mistake next time?' Parents must also try to discern where jealousy is causing the problem and find ways of reassuring the child who feels neglected or inferior.

Relationships with people outside the family circle

All that happens within the home will help or hinder our children from being friendly and making and keeping friends. We can further encourage them by being glad to have their friends in for meals and to play. Little by little and tactfully, i.e. not in front of their friends, we can teach them useful social skills, such as how to share, take turns, be polite and have good manners. These things, at least in my experience, do not necessarily come naturally!

The loner

Some children do seem reluctant to make friends. These are sometimes only children, but loners can also come from bigger families. Such children seem to prefer their own company or that of adults to the companionship of their peers.

It's a great shame for children to miss out on the joys of friendship, but we cannot force the issue. It's important to discover whether a child is a loner from choice, and perfectly happy about the situation, or from lack of confidence in himself and fear of others. If the latter, some of the suggestions in this book about helping children to face life confidently and courageously might be useful. Perhaps all we can do for the loner-by-choice is to pray that God will cause the circumstances in his life to wean him away from self-sufficiency – which is a pretty limiting outlook – and towards others whom he may need without knowing it, or who may need him.

Trial friendships

Friends are important to our children from about the age of three onwards, but for several years there will be a good deal of chopping and changing, as they sort out whom they really like. It's probably wise not to act immediately when our children choose unhelpful friends at this age, because the chances are that things will sort themselves out before too long. If not, we could invite other, more helpful, friends to tea and influence matters in ways such as that!

Deeper friendships

From eleven onwards, our children will be relying more and more on their friends. We need to avoid feeling resentful, and be actively interested without crowding them in this area.

Undesirable friendships at this age and stage are more serious because they may well be more lasting and influential.

But a little parental honesty is needed before we take action. Are we wanting to interfere in a friendship because our child's friend is socially different from him, or because we genuinely believe spiritual and moral issues are involved?

If we are sure that our child is being led astray, how should we react? By prayer, direct action or subtlety?

Once again, we need to know our child. The direct approach – saying why we disapprove of the friendship and giving our advice or instructions about it – could cause hurt and resentment ('rejecting my friend is like rejecting me'). So we might have to talk to God rather than to the child about the matter. On the other hand, direct parental intervention is sometimes exactly what the child needs and wants.

I was not a strong-willed child and another boy latched on to me mainly so that I would do his homework for him every night and also to gratify his desire to have a hold over someone weaker.

On one occasion, I deliberately stayed at his home, helping him to do his homework until I had missed my piano lesson. I hoped that as a result, my parents would forbid me to see him or take some similar action, which would have helped me to break away – but they didn't and much sadness resulted. (Alexander)

Clearly, parents need the wisdom of Solomon, but friendship is such a beautiful gift of God that we will want to do everything we can to help our children to enjoy it.

Encouraging Christian friendships

The friendships which ought to be of a very special quality indeed are those between Christians. In adolescence, the formation of strong Christian friendships can make all the difference. In fact, without the backing of like-minded peers, it's unlikely that our young people will be able to withstand the enormous inner and social pressures on them to conform to the majority. Those who don't sleep around, take drugs, go to all-night drinking parties and the like, could well be teased or ostracised and this *hurts*. If we are asking our adolescents to be different, we are expecting a very great deal of them, and we need to appreciate this. The least we can do, therefore, is to make sure that they are part of a strong, well-organised, well-taught church youth group, and pray, very hard, that they will make helpful friendships within it. If we are also willing to make our homes available at times to our young people and their friends – albeit with suitable rules, e.g. no drugs, and all washing-up to be done by those who used the things – that could be productive. For children brought up in Christian homes, adolescence and young adulthood are often make-or-break times in their spiritual lives, so it's worth doing all we can to be supportive.

Friendships leading to marriage

Ideally, young people need to have a wide circle of friends of both sexes for many years before they start pairing off. Parents can help by having open house as often as possible, and by encouraging discussion on whatever interests their young people.

> We talk about everything with our son – VD, contraception, pre-marital sex, abortion. These are live issues for most teenagers today. We talk from a Christian viewpoint and point up the issues for and against. Final choices must be his. (Dawn)

> Christian attitudes to sex are born of open, healthy home relationships and much unplanned, open discussion on

friendships and moral issues as they relate to people one reads about or knows. (Mary)

The value of open dialogue between parents and young people cannot be over-emphasised. Parents must make the matter of their children's future partners the focus of constant prayer. If teenagers and parents could pray together about these things, this would be very beneficial. But not all teenagers or parents can manage this without embarrassment or strain. In some cases, another adult can be a great help – youth leader, godparent, relative or friend. Whoever they are, we should trust and pray for them and conquer any resentment we may feel that our child should prefer to talk to them rather than to us. Even where there is a good relationship, some teenagers find it easier to talk to adults other than their parents about certain matters – and we should be happy for this to happen.

As well as informal discussion at home and elsewhere, clear biblical teaching is needed on topics such as guidance, marriage and relationships. Also, relevant psychological insights on temperament, men and women, and emotions are important.

In all these ways our young people can develop healthy attitudes towards the opposite sex and marriage. But perhaps the most formative influence of all upon them in this area will be the quality of our (their parents') marriage relationship.

AFFECTION

I am certain that demonstrative, affectionate love plays a very vital part in building a sense of worth in a child.

Showing affection to young children

Unlike God, small children judge by appearances. Time and again I have heard one or other of them remark that a particular adult was cross with them or didn't like them and discovered that their reason for concluding this was that the adult in question didn't *smile*. Just that!

Young children need to *see* that we love them by our smiling faces, *hear* that we love them by our tone of voice as well as by our words, and *feel* that we love them by our kisses and hugs and the way we touch and hold them.

When they are older, they will be able to read between the lines and infer that we love them from the fact that we do things for them, or from cryptic comments and subtle changes in our voices or expressions. But for many years prior to that they will need more specific, tangible, visible, audible evidence of our feelings.

Some parents, for a variety of reasons, find it hard to express deep feelings so plainly, but if they do not overcome their reluctance in this, both they and their children will be the losers. Love expressed and demonstrated affectionately is joyful, healing and reassuring. Partners who have discovered this in their own relationship will be able to show affection more readily to their children than those who have not.

Showing affection to older children

As we said, older children can read love in other ways, but that's no reason to stop showing affection to them. I am sorry that in the West, tradition has it that fathers should not hug their adolescent sons – but do Christians have to accept such a tradition? Of course, we have to be sensitive to our children's feelings and refrain from affectionate responses if these are causing them embarrassment. But otherwise, so much is to be gained through members of families feeling free to be affectionate with one another.

Every aspect of love that we show to our children brings added richness to their concept of God's love when they are taught about that. There is great affection in God's love for us even though he does not, generally speaking, express it through physical touch. But Jesus certainly loved through touch, and we can encourage our children for this reason, too, to be affectionate.

UNDERSTANDING

We must take the trouble to understand children in general at every age and stage, and our children in particular. We cannot all become experts on child development, but we must at least know the fundamentals. Most people who are presented with a new plant or strange animal will take the trouble to find out a bit about it and perhaps get a book from the library about how to take care of it. Strangely enough, many parents assume that bringing up a child will come naturally to them and that it's almost an insult to suggest they might like to read a book or two on the subject.

Yet children are far more intricate and complex than any plant or animal and the necessary skill and knowledge are not automatically given to parents along with their little one. We must be prepared to do a little reading up! It's absurd to think otherwise.

At the same time, we shouldn't necessarily follow the experts' advice to the letter, but rather use it as a guide to aid us in understanding our unique son or daughter. We cannot become experts on *all* children, but it's our job to learn to be experts on *our* children – with a view to handling them wisely and well.

When we show our children that we know how they feel and why, and realise what caused them to behave in certain ways, they will begin to feel understood. I have often made the mistake of trying to rationalise a situation when a child comes in feeling angry or hurt, but am learning that the number one thing to do is to identify with his feelings and show sympathy and understanding. *Afterwards*, he may be able to receive advice and comments, or even offer them himself, but *always* empathy with and the support of the person should come *first*.

We must understand our baby's need for constant care, the emotional tug-of-war that often takes place inside our toddlers, the fantasy world of our children, and our adolescents' sexuality, questions, doubts and fears – and find ways of showing and telling them that we do. This presupposes that we love our children enough to give them time and take trouble over them.

Time and love

> 'Your children . . . are holy.' (1 Cor. 7:14). But they will not turn out that way if they are given money and toys instead of love and time. If parents fail to encourage, discipline and apologise to their young, they need not be surprised if they turn out to be a disappointment; likewise if the parents are out at church meetings several nights a week.[1]

True understanding comes from seeing a child with perceptive, compassionate love. Much of this book is about various aspects of genuine love and how to show and encourage it, but it's worth saying something here about the love that gives time.

There is absolutely no substitute for spending time with our children and failing to do this might be a cause for bitter regrets later. Parental time is usually spent generously on young children, but as they grow older, it becomes all too possible to spend less and less time with them. They may not require us to do things for them, but they still need us to listen. This is essential if we are going to understand them and to help them to feel understood. Paul Tournier has written that it is impossible to over-emphasise the immense need humans have to be really listened to, to be taken

1. Michael Green, *To Corinth With Love* (Hodder & Stoughton).

seriously, to be understood. 'No one can develop freely in this world and find life without feeling understood by at least one person.' General family times, such as meals and outings, are very useful but there is much value in a parent spending time alone with each child.

> We try to keep in mind a suggestion made by one Christian writer – that each parent should spend one hour per week with each child doing something special. (Penny)

Keeping to such a plan would need determination and self-discipline, but what better way of telling a child that he's special and valued as an individual? And what are we telling him, if we *don't* spend time with him?

> A well-known Christian leader said to me, with tears in his eyes, that his grown-up son had said to him, 'In all my childhood, you only found time to go fishing with me twice.' (Cyril)

How much time?

None of us would want to spend too little time with our children – but is it possible to lavish too much time and attention on them? I believe it is, and that we must sort out our priorities – God first, our partners next and then, jointly, the children. Idolising, being sentimental about or too wrapped up in our children, as well as worrying incessantly about and over-protecting them, is bad for them and for us. On some children, the effects of these attitudes can be as harmful as the effects of neglect and lack of care.

God's understanding

If our children feel understood, but not crowded by or chained to us, they will more readily respond to teaching about God's perfect and total understanding of them.

ENCOURAGEMENT

The songwriter's 'home on the range' might be a place 'where seldom is heard a discouraging word', but I'm afraid the same could not be said of every Christian home.

I think especially of our niece. Her parents and brothers have so often said, 'She's no good at anything,' that she now believes them. I once commended her on a lovely card she had made, saying, 'I think this is beautiful! You know, you're really very artistic!' but her mother chipped in with, 'Oh, she isn't really!' (Tina)

I wonder when we last encouraged our children for:
- accepting a 'No,' with a good grace
- sharing, helping, obeying/willingly
- showing gentleness to someone weaker and smaller
- treating callers politely, especially when they interrupted their favourite television programmes
- remembering to thank someone for doing something for them
- owning up, saying sorry and forgiving/of their own accord
- keeping a promise
- coping with something they found hard without a fuss
- being thoughtful.

A simple 'Well done/Thank you/That was kind/I was proud of you!' can boost a flagging ego, together with a hug or kiss. But sometimes a little surprise or reward might be added. Money and sweets are easily overdone, so some other gift could be considered, or a treat such as an outing or letting them invite a friend to a meal or for the night.

I am convinced that we need to praise, reward, encourage and commend our children far more than we do for every effort they make to do right or be co-operative.

Some children appear to have been indiscriminately encouraged, like the small boy who was discovered helping himself to the sugar while reiterating, presumably between mouthfuls, 'Mummy's good boy.' But mostly we err the other way – not commenting when all is calm and the children are fitting in well, but very quick to scold, nag or shout when they rock the boat a fraction.

The atmosphere in a home can be revolutionised when parents are on the look-out for all they can praise in their children's words, actions or attitudes. Perhaps many of us need to learn from that great encourager, Barnabas (Acts 4:36; 11:23; 14:22).

Older children need encouragement just as much as, if not more than, younger ones. James Dobson writes: 'I have observed that the vast majority of those between twelve and twenty years are bitterly disappointed with who they are and what they represent.'[2] If James Dobson is right, and if we don't want our young people to be among the discouraged majority, we will need to feed in massive encouragement as well as using all the other means of building up a sense of worth and significance in them.

We mustn't be deceived by a cocksure manner; it does not necessarily indicate confidence and inner security. Even those who are outwardly coping, may well need encouragement and support as they try to discover who they are and what they want to do.

Avoid negative comments

It's so easy to get into the habit of talking about our children in front of them when they are young. It would be much better not to do this at all, and certainly to avoid negative comments such as:

- Peter never gets to sleep before one o'clock
- I can't get Jill to clean her teeth properly
- Paul won't eat vegetables
- Sandy and Alison simply don't get on: they fight all the time

2. James Dobson, *Hide or Seek* (Hodder & Stoughton).

- Sue's bad-tempered in the mornings
- John's a cry-baby
- I dread taking Becky to the dentist/doctor: she always makes such a fuss
- Bryn's anti-social – a hopeless mixer
- Don takes hours to get dressed
- Petra will show off in front of visitors.

Though these comments may be strictly, or almost, accurate, they are not helpful. First, they are disloyal. Second, they would tend to confirm to the child his negative characteristic rather than giving him the hope or confidence to move towards a more positive one. Also, some of the statements imply that the child is in control of the parent – which ought not to be the case.

So if we are going to talk about the child in his hearing, let's say things that are going to give him a positive self-image.

As well as encouraging our children by every human means possible, we can teach them to draw strength and encouragement from God as David did (1 Sam. 30:7) and from his many promises, including this marvellous one: 'We know that in all things God works for the good of those who love him, who have been called according to his purpose.' (Rom. 8:28).

ENJOYMENT

It's very important for children to feel that their parents actually enjoy playing with them, talking and listening to them. We can start assuring them along these lines very early on in their lives.

Make sure that some time, say half an hour each day is given to playing or romping at the child's level, i.e. on the floor. Later on any older children in the family will take an active interest in this. Our two boys loved inventing games for their little sister and she learnt while still young to move counters round boards, etc.

Children also need to play outdoors in open country where they can be energetic and noisy if they want to be. Activities such as building dams in mountain streams to produce paddling pools for younger children can be marvellous opportunities for learning, talking, developing team spirit and just having fun with our children. (Hugh)

As children grow older, stocks of indoor and outdoor games can be very useful for evenings and holiday times.

Shared hobbies and interests can also be another source of fun between parents and children at weekends and other times. Swimming, fishing, collecting things, nature study, cooking, camping, books, walking, music, art, craft, sport and other activities can all be fun, but parents have to be very careful not to kill the interest for the child by expecting too much and overdoing things.

I've learnt much about steam trains and we are discovering the coins of the world. With one son we discovered birds, then we went into stones, semi-precious gems and geology and have discovered wonders galore between agate and zircon. After that came wild flowers so that our country walks have become even more delightful as we spot and try to name the miniature wonders. (Hugh)

I seldom say, 'Why not do some painting?' but, 'I saw a lovely scene today and I'm dying to paint it,' and then get out the paints – and my daughter is soon joining in. I'm not even a dabbler – just an O Level Art failure, but I love colours. If one genuinely enjoys something, it usually rubs off on one's children. (Beth)

Meals can be great times too, when everyone can share news, laugh, joke, tease and generally have fun – provided one eats away from the television!

As families grow together they gain a sense of identity, so a child can say, 'Our family does this, but not that.' In a family that takes time to relax and play together regularly, the sense of identity can have happy connotations. Jokes, stories, sayings, can pass into family lore and be repeated often. Traditions, such as fish-and-chips on the lounge floor on Saturdays, can grow up and be enjoyed by all, provided no one feels cramped or threatened by them.

It would be unrealistic to suggest that family life is all fun and games. Clearly, sadness, conflict and anxiety will occur. But if it's within our power to do so, we should try to ensure that there are more happy, harmonious family times than unhappy, fraught ones. Then children will have a 'good feeling' about their homes.

It's vitally important that we should enjoy our children and that they should know that we do, and that God enjoys their company too and wants to share their joys and sorrows.

If we *don't* enjoy our children's company, why not? If it's because we are embarrassed by their bad behaviour, then the chances are other people won't enjoy their company either. The future will then look rather bleak for them, socially. Spoilt, greedy, rude, selfish children are a joy to no one, so we will have to take action for our children's, if not our own, sake.

SUCCESS

Human beings need 'to struggle, to plan ahead, to battle towards a difficult goal, and then to enjoy the conquest'.[3]

In order to achieve our potential, we need to be stretched – but not too much or too often, and this stretching needs to lead to some degree of success, or we become too discouraged to go on trying.

I believe it's very important to our children to succeed in

3. Evelyn Peterson, *Who Cares?* (Paternoster).

some area that gives them a sense of worth and some standing in the eyes of their peers and friends. It's good for a child to be able to say, 'I am good at swimming, tennis, dancing,' or whatever.

Fortunately, many children do have at least one obvious talent which gives them as much success and kudos as they need. But there are others who seem to be average or poor at most things and, before they are very old, they can easily have a generalised feeling of failure and hopelessness about themselves. I think wise and loving parents need to work very hard to help such children succeed at something, as soon as possible.

We have a child who had educational problems and was not competitive or good enough to show up well on the sports field either. So we found one thing that she could do better than others and have encouraged, pushed and prodded her in this area. Frequently – the moment the work becomes hard – she has wanted to give up – but we have felt it right to urge her to keep at it. Another interest emerged and we have done the same thing in this area, too. We think that success and encouragement in these fields, i.e. ballet and cookery, have boosted her confidence in other areas too. (Di)

Teaching them what true success means

We don't want our children to gain the impression that their worth depends on the things they are good at. So alongside helping them to succeed at something, we will need to teach them:

- that they do not have to succeed, or do anything else, *for us*
- that we love them for themselves, not for what they achieve, and so does God
- that doing their best is good enough for us and for God
- that God's idea of success is quite different from that of

society (he doesn't regard brains, beauty, athletic ability, fame or wealth as any criteria at all)

- that they can be successful with God the moment they ask Jesus to be their Saviour and Lord and let his Spirit start making them more like him.

It's no good telling our children these things if our actions cancel out our message. For instance, if we tell our children that if they do their best in exams, that's good enough for us – but promise them the earth if they pass, or panic like mad when the results are due to arrive, they are hardly likely to believe us, and rightly.

Do we really, genuinely, want our children to succeed with God or do we also add the proviso that they get a respectable number of O and A Levels followed by a 'good' (in terms of money and status) job? We must be prepared to lay aside all preconceptions, including family traditions such as, 'In our family the oldest son always becomes a stockbroker,' and pray that our children will please God first and foremost, whether this will mean 'losing their lives' in a needy part of his world or emptying dustbins in Golders Green.

So, to help build up our child's sense of worth, we may need to work hard to make it possible for him to succeed at something, but at the same time we will be feeding in God's view of the matter and encouraging him to 'seek first his kingdom and his righteousness' (Matt. 6:33), and turn his back on what the world regards as great.

FAIRNESS

'Why bother?' would be some people's reaction to the suggestion that we should treat our children fairly.

A friend of ours said, 'I never try to even out what I give to my children. Life is unfair and they may as well accept it from the beginning.' (Hugh)

I don't think it's right to take this cavalier attitude, because we are supposed to pattern our parenting on God and he is perfectly fair and just. We certainly can't be totally fair at all times, but it's important to try – and admit failure when it happens.

Avoiding favouritism

One very common failing is favouritism, dating back at least as far as patriarchal times. Think of Rebecca and Jacob, Isaac and Esau, Jacob and Joseph! We are just as human and prone to error as they were. We may feel very drawn to one child and find another hard to like, perhaps because he has characteristics we dislike – too much like our own, possibly? – or because he doesn't respond well to us. If we do dislike a child, it might be good to do all or some of these things:

- admit our feelings to ourselves and to God, to our partner and perhaps also to a trusted friend
- pray for love (God definitely can give us love for a child we don't like)
- pray for the child daily until things improve, including being thankful for every one of his God-given characteristics
- look out daily for anything commendable the child does and praise him for it
- keep trusting God to bring good out of this situation (after all, it has already caused you to pray more than you would have for the child, and that can't be bad!).

Teaching and showing them what true fairness is

Our children's justice is not always as informed or objective as it might be! So we may need to draw attention, gently, to some blind spots. For instance, if a child resents the fact that we bought his sister a new skirt, we may have to remind him of the shoes he was given not long before. But children are not the only ones with blind spots, and as our children mature, they will see us more realistically. If so, would we allow them to tell us a few home truths in the right spirit?

In older adolescence when abstracts such as equality can be understood, it should be possible to show that fairness isn't always achieved by giving everyone exactly the same treatment, because people's needs are different. Therefore it might be perfectly fair to give one child more help with something than another.

God's kind of fairness

That God is completely fair is something we can teach young children (Isa. 61:8) but as they grow they will look around and see apparent examples of his unfairness everywhere (Ps. 37:35). If we're honest we will have to agree that life's justice does look very rough and that some of the best people seem to suffer most. But we have to trust God's word that he *is* just and in control, and that ultimately he will judge the world and the people in it with perfect fairness (Acts 17:31; 1 Cor. 4:5).

The Bible outlook is that if God were to give us what we truly deserved, he would have to condemn us to death and hell. Instead, because of Jesus's perfect sacrifice, he can still be just while offering us forgiveness and a new start (Rom. 3:21–26). We cannot explain these mysteries to our older children, but we can share the truths and pray for the Holy Spirit's faith-producing activity in them.

BELONGING AND BEING NEEDED

We all need to feel that we belong and have a part to play. How can we help each child to feel welcome and needed in the family and the life of the home?

Giving each child a suitable Saturday job is one sugges-tion. When children are small they will probably do little tasks for us quite happily, but juniors may well be reluctant helpers or even very bolshy. But it's important that they should contribute – not only to give them a sense of being needed, but also to teach them that privileges bring responsibilities. It's worth weathering some nasty scenes to bring this about.

If we remember to thank them for doing the jobs each time and say how much we appreciate their help, the atmosphere will probably improve in time!

Another idea is to do a little detailed forward planning so that each child is given a share of the action when there are family fun evenings, e.g. at Christmas and birthdays, or a bit of responsibility when there are special events to prepare for or outings to plan.

Very often we could do the job we ask the child to do in half the time and very much better. But we will have to learn patience and self-control and let the child do it. If by these and other ways our children do start to take responsibility and to realise that their contribution is important, then it shouldn't be too hard for them to accept that God has a place for them in his family and a part for them to play in his world.

CONTROL AND FREEDOM

Children need older, wiser people in charge of them, laying down the limits, organising, overseeing and helping. In the beginning, we have to do virtually everything for our babies, but gradually our role will change. Instead of doing things for the child, we will more and more enable him to manage his own affairs. But total freedom will not be granted until he is, or ought to be, ready for it.

Parents and other experts

As our children grow, all sorts of other influences and people come into their lives – friends, schools, teachers, clubs and club leaders, church and church leaders, dentists, doctors, careers officers, and the like. We will be delegating various aspects of our children's upbringing or care to these people or establishments, while remaining in overall charge. Many experts have much to offer our children, but they shouldn't be allowed to usurp or undermine parental authority.

Parents should be very willing to accept insights offered by people with specialised knowledge or skills. Equally, the experts should be prepared to concede that parents are, or ought to be, experts as far as knowing and understanding their unique child is concerned. Both should work together in any situation that concerns the child.

Unfortunately there has been a tendency lately for some experts to deal with children as isolated units and to treat their parents as irrelevant or even a nuisance. This attitude has angered many capable parents and caused less capable ones to lose any shred of confidence they may have managed to retain. Ideally, specialists should see part of their role as enabling parents to do their job better and more wisely and confidently.

In practice, experts can seem pretty formidable to parents. We may need considerable courage to stand up to them when we feel it is in our child's best interests to do so. But we must try hard not to be aggressive; it's possible to be firm and courteous at the same time, and this usually achieves more than rudeness.

Sleeping problems

Rebecca and Ray were willing to listen to the experts with regard to their children's sleeping problems. Their experiences may not by typical, but their comments should be helpful to many.

Both Mandy and Charles were totally unsettled from the moment of birth until about two and a half years old. The cumulative effect was five years of extremely interrupted nights. We have wondered whether this was due in part to their being bottle fed and having digestive problems; both certainly suffered from nightmares.

The following solutions were put to us by doctors, health visitors, friends and relatives. We were willing to try *anything*!

- Let them cry themselves to sleep; they're playing up; establish the upper hand; shut the door and turn up the wireless. Result: Both children were violently sick and became disturbed during the day as well. We concluded that the above ideas were not workable in the case of highly imaginative children.

- Leave a light on. (Using a dim light cuts down the cost – and it could perhaps be the hall rather than the bedroom light.) This certainly assisted the wakeful night hours and rendered them horror free. There does seem to be an inbuilt horror of the dark with some children even before images of wolves, ghosts, etc. are picked up from books. (Ray's marginal comment: We both believe that witch and ghost stories, however comical, are basically anti-Christian, and that the devil should not be made a subject for jokes. Such books therefore are banned.)

  N.B. Charles was a difficult pregnancy. Referring to his whereabouts before birth he insists, 'It was dark in there and I was cold.'

- Close the curtains. This helped Mandy because she thought people were looking in at her and she didn't like the idea. When I was small, and even as a teenager, I was terrified of drawn-back curtains at night, but my mother insisted on this; also I was not allowed a light and this certainly gave me bad dreams.

- Give drinks. We found that a nice warm bottle did soothe the child. Some people might say that the child will wake for the drink, but we found that on the rare good night, a bottle placed by the bed was not touched.

81

We kept a thermos of warm water to save going for the kettle. They gradually accepted cool and then cold drinks which needed no assistance.

- Use a dummy. What would we do without them?! We found them invaluable, and easy to keep clean. We didn't pin these to their clothing, but bought a dozen and handed out a new one when the previous one disappeared. If I could have got over my psychological block about dummies sooner (and people can be very scathing about them, while thumb sucking seems acceptable) I think Mandy would have settled much more quickly. We thought she might suffocate or that it might be bad for her teeth. When Charles arrived, we were too exhausted to remove the dummy from her mouth, and she improved – obviously needing that sort of comfort.

- Use drugs? We were pressed to use sedatives but neither of us could come to terms with this. As a matter of principle, I felt I could not take the risk of being responsible for artificially altering a small child's thought processes and possibly retard him for life – in order to benefit myself. Maybe I would have thought differently if I had had a nervous breakdown. As it is, with physical weakness resulting from those years, I don't regret the non-use of drugs at all. A little boy I know well who was a non-sleeper was drugged for about six to seven years and it has definitely affected him. Parents have to decide for themselves on these matters.

- Alter sleeping arrangements. As a last resort, we moved the beds about and one parent had a good night's sleep whilst the other had a bad one. This was not an ideal solution: the sleeper felt wretched for the non-sleeper and it was impossible to deaden all sound. But it did save our sanity at times.

- Place large soothing pictures at the foot of the bed. This lessened Mandy's nightmares dramatically. She had a beautiful poster of a child her own age picking flowers in a field, and would spend hours gazing at her friend.

As well as the helpful suggestions above, it's good to have a winding-down routine which the baby comes to associate as soon as possible with sleep. This could involve putting him in his cot, making him comfortable and secure – some babies respond very well to being really firmly wrapped up – darkening the room, talking quietly, refusing to play peekaboo, and leaving the room calmly but quickly.

Our mental attitude is also important. Keep it firmly in mind that you, the parents, are in charge and expect your child to accept your wise, loving control. Remember, too, that broken nights do not last for ever – it only seems that way! While they do last, we need all the help we can get – from God, our partner, friends and experts – in order to survive ourselves while trying to handle the situation in such a way that our child will feel that we love him, understand his needs and fears, and are in charge.

Schools

Education is another area in which we need to be in charge – choosing and delegating wisely and then staying actively involved.

Our first choice, if we are fortunate, will be whether or not to send our child to a pre-school group and if so, what sort. Then comes 'big school'. In theory, we can choose what schools we send our children to. In practice, whether we have any choice at all is probably dependent on where we live and the size of our bank balance.

We say we want a good school for our child, but often what we really mean is that we want an academic education for him: intellectual abilities, and prestigious jobs are still considered 'the tops' by most people. But surely this is worldly and not biblical thinking at all. A good school for our child must be the one that suits him best – a place where he is stretched but not struggling desperately. Long-term relationships and attitudes are more important than qualifications, and therefore when we choose a school, the quality of the teachers and the atmosphere should be at least as important to us as the exam results.

Being an involved and helpful parent

It's very important to establish a good relationship with our children's teachers, and to show that we're prepared to give as well as take. Little gestures such as contributing good Christian books to the library could generate much goodwill and perhaps shed a little light too! Trusting, backing up and praying for our children's teachers will help everyone far more than criticising them, hogging too much of their time and seeing them only in relation to our own children, rather than as people in their own right with a hard job to do.

Staying involved through secondary school education

Parents sometimes tail off in interest and involvement as their children leave primary and junior schools and go on to secondary education. But parental involvement and interest is absolutely crucial during these years. The old-style head – whose personality permeated the whole school and shaped quite considerably the teaching and behaviour of the staff – is largely extinct, at least within the state system. Individual teachers are given greater freedom to teach and behave as they think fit. Such freedom is good where teachers are dedicated, high-principled people; but otherwise, unsatisfactory situations can occur.

We are horrified, and rightly so, at the repressive and harsh discipline that existed in some Victorian schools, but I wonder whether a severe caning, even if unjustly inflicted, caused anything like the damage that must surely result from situations such as the following, all of which occurred at a secondary modern school with a good reputation:

- a master suspected of homosexuality and made the butt of jokes by masters to pupils
- masters cracking obscene jokes and swearing at pupils
- pupils hitting masters
- a master telling his examination candidates, 'Frankly, I couldn't care less whether you pass or not.'

Reacting in a Christian and wise manner

If things like these are going on at our children's schools, we have to be aware of them. Then we have to think very hard about what action to take. Some parents may feel it's right to remove a child from such a situation, but there is no perfect school anywhere and even if there were, our son or daughter would have to face an imperfect world afterwards. Probably our best policy would be to enable our children to cope with these things in such a way as to develop strength of character and Christian attitudes.

We may also find a way of improving the situation, but we will need to be very low key and tactful so as not to antagonise the school or cause embarrassment to our child. Writing shocked, condemnatory, self-righteous letters may make us feel better but they don't usually influence others for good. We need to be sure that our motive for doing anything is that the situation will be improved and not that we will be seen to be in the right.

The parents below decided to take direct action in the situations confronting their children. What would you have done in their shoes?

Our daughter has a reading problem, but having told the teachers at her secondary school about this and knowing that the primary school had passed on information to that effect, we felt confident that all would be well. So we were upset when our daughter came home in tears and said that the RE teacher had asked her to stand up and read out a Bible passage and had then commented unfavourably on her stumbling efforts to do so. We went to see the first year head about this matter as we felt it was worth making a point about vital information about children being passed on to all those involved in teaching them. In this instance, lack of communication and/or sensitivity had unnecessarily humiliated a child in an area in which she was already very vulnerable – and the teacher had lost out on her objective, which was presumably that the passage should be read out well and clearly.

We also had to point out that poor spellers and writers like our daughter found it impossible to take down homework that was flung out by teachers verbally on their way to the door at the end of a lesson, that the ensuing hieroglyphics could be totally indecipherable – and that much misery could be avoided if teachers would write the homework on the board and give children time to take it down. (Di)

Soon after our son went to senior school, a master ridiculed him in class by reading out his essay strictly according to punctuation. My wife wrote a well-composed note in the book below the essay and the master was as good as gold after that. (Alexander)

Some comfort?

God can bring good out of all our children's school problems. Many parents have found this to be true.

We have certainly had a lot of anxiety over our children's education, but the fact that the schools weren't brilliant meant that we had to keep far more continuously in touch with what was going on than would have been the case if we had had more confidence in the system. (Lisa)

Homework

Here's what some parents have to say about this:

We asked our son how he felt homework was best coped with and he said, 'Get on with it as soon as possible, so you can enjoy your free time.' Both the boys are happier if they manage to do this.

We have a drink and sandwich available when they arrive home and then they change clothes and settle down. Difficulties arise when parents are not around to encourage self-discipline. Doing set pieces doesn't present problems, but learning and revising are different, because they tend to think they've done it after spending five minutes or so reading the work through. Parents need the discipline and patience to sit with the children, listen, test and so on; also a good encyclopedia or a nearby library to help with all the impossible questions for which answers are wanted now if not sooner! (Hugh)

We feel strongly that it's good to encourage our children to do what they can but never bring too much pressure to bear. The home should be the place where the child can find a refuge from the pressures which school and peers put on him, and total acceptance. (Mary)

By the age of twelve, we expected the children to be motivated to do their own homework and to bear the worry and responsibility of not doing it or not doing it well. This didn't mean we weren't interested or didn't give help; we were and we very often did. But it did mean that we expected the children to come to us for help, rather than us fussing over them to see that they had done what they should.

I much preferred my child to go to school with bad work and incur the wrath of the teacher and the disciplinary process of the school, than to mask the situation by too much help or prodding from me. (Prue)

Giving suitable refreshment, being available, and helping *just enough* seem to be important. High homework marks that are mostly the fruit of Mum's or Dad's labours are not much help to the child long term. Our real aim should be to help him to develop good attitudes, and the ability to concentrate and organise himself and his work.

As always, knowing one's child is crucial. A few children seem to develop the right approach to work without much bother, but most seem to swing too far towards either an over-conscientious or a slap-happy attitude. Some of our friends seem to spend their time urging their children to be a bit easier on themselves and to relax more, while the others are obliged to prod their easy-going under-achievers into working harder and caring more!

Sex education

Parents do need to be in charge and aware of what's happening in the area of their children's sex education. If we don't tell our children what we want them to know *before* puberty, another child will almost certainly enlighten them far less satisfactorily.

Nor can we leave it all to the school, because sex education there isn't always very good or complete. For one thing, such talks seem to take place in the context of science and science laboratories – with all their not necessarily helpful connotations! For another, moral and ethical considerations may not even be mentioned, any more than the thoughts, feelings, intentions, imagination, expectations and all the other things which give the sexual act its distinctively human quality, over and above the mere physical act.

Is there anything we can do to encourage schools which give the bare facts, without any warmth or reference to the crucial human side, to rethink their policy? It would be better, for instance, if 'sex lessons' were part of an RE or humanities course, where the focus at least is on people.

As Christian parents, we will want additionally to put sex into a spiritual context, and, along with the local church, to teach biblical principles such as pre-marital chastity and faithfulness within marriage. We need also, in these days, to emphasise that divorce is as devastating and extreme as amputation, since husband and wife are 'one flesh' (Mark 10:7).

Juniors, and perhaps Primaries too, often ask very direct questions on sexual matters, and we need to answer them openly and sensitively, stressing that sex isn't just about 'getting a baby' but about feeling, loving, sharing and giving.

In adolescence the biblical and psychological principles need to be spelt out very clearly, so that young people understand what God's standards are as well as the differences between men and women and the part that feelings, memories, thoughts, expectations, imagination and past experiences play in the sexual act.

I think we need to strike a balance between being too serious or matter-of-fact about these matters, and too solemn or idealistic. A sense of humour can be a help here. The humour I am thinking of is not a cheapening and degradation of sex, but a way of coming to terms with the gap between the ideal and the actual: between what one feels and imagines about the sexual act and what it symbolises, and one's rather inept attempt to express it physically. C. S. Lewis was probably right to point out that our frail, fallible human bodies have a touch of the buffoon about them, and certainly right to warn us against idolising erotic love. So if a joke about sex comes up which isn't offensive, and is funny, there's no reason why we shouldn't laugh at it with our teenagers. But this is a very different matter from seeing sexual love as one big joke.

Balancing freedom and control is one of the main themes of this book. Our aim is to protect the child from what he cannot cope with while enabling him to handle what he can and so to mature as a person and a Christian. Not that our children always see eye to eye with us on all our decisions!

When our daughter was thirteen, some school friends asked her to join them on a picnic one Sunday afternoon. Knowing the youngsters involved, I was very uneasy about the plan and told my daughter so. She objected very plainly to having a far-too-fussy mum. In the end I said, 'You can go if you promise you'll be home by 6 p.m.' She agreed and I watched her pedal off with some misgivings, since I sensed that the other children – one boy and two girls, all much older – wanted to get away from parental protection for their own rather doubtful ends.

At 6 p.m. my daughter came home breathless and tearful. She hadn't even eaten her picnic lunch. Later, when she had calmed down she said, 'Mum, I'm so glad you said I had to be home by six o'clock because then I could tell the others I had to leave. I just left them behind on the hills and came home as fast as I could. I felt afraid to be on my own with them.'

I learnt from this incident that I have to let my children go with certain safeguards, and my daughter learnt that while independence seems attractive, it does have certain drawbacks and risks and parental safeguards can be a great help here. (Denise)

We want the best for our children, but we often have to let them find out the hard way, through trial and error, what the best is. Also we must be very sure that we don't confuse what's best for our children with what *we* want them to do. It is *their* potential, not our dreams, that we should want them to realise.

My father was interested in languages and tried, unsuccessfully, to make his daughters into linguists. Also, my sister and I knew for many years exactly what we wanted to do, but Father was determined that we should follow his and Mother's footsteps into the 'sacred profession' (i.e. teaching), and that nothing else would do. When we stuck out against this, we finished up working in an office which we both found pretty loathsome and dull and no outlet for our particular talents. The result has been a lasting feeling of bitterness and resentment against parental domination. (Tina)

Obviously, there is nothing wrong with parents trying to guide their children or pass on their own interests and enthusiasms to them, but this is a very different thing from forcing them into our moulds. In a choice of career, the child's gifts and interests have to come first.

Setting them free completely

'The parental purpose should be to grant increasing freedom and responsibility year by year, so that when the child gets beyond adult control, he will no longer need it.'[4]

Letting go is a long, slow process but when the time comes for the child to take responsibility for his own life, many parents find it very hard indeed. Some simply cannot bear to lose their offspring and others cannot trust them. I have heard of several parents who are hanging on to their children and letting them do things they don't approve of, because they are afraid of what might happen if they were left entirely to their own devices away from home. Perhaps they are right to do this and perhaps their children are not ready for freedom. But in that case, shouldn't they respect their parents' wishes?

4. James Dobson, *Discipline While You Can* (Kingsway).

It must be very hard for people in such situations. They are in charge of their homes and responsible for what happens there (see the householder's responsibility for everyone living on his property, right down to his manservant, maidservant and animals – Exod. 20:10). But they also feel responsible for their children, and don't want to alienate them by making them conform to their standards.

Each parent must decide what to do about an unhappy state of affairs like this, should it arise, but it's obvious that we cannot protect our children for ever from the consequences of their own actions. It could be argued that having to take responsibility, make their own decisions, manage their own affairs and generally behave like adults might jolt them into more mature, sensible behaviour.

When they do leave the nest, if we really do set them free, they will probably come back willingly and often to us, and the relationship can become increasingly one of friendship where we advise and help only when asked to. Trusting God for these new young adults and showing trust towards them are far, far better than being over-anxious and still trying to manage things, thus probably undermining their confidence and causing resentment.

With God's help, even our imperfect handling of our children can influence them towards choosing to put themselves into God's perfectly wise and perfectly loving control, and opting for the perfect freedom of his service.

IDENTITY

Think of yourself with sober judgment, in accordance with the measure of faith God has given you. (Rom. 12:3).

'The good experiences from the past (one's roots) are combined with the expectations for the future (one's goals) to produce a sense of self-worth. This self-worth is the basis for the ongoing awareness of self – an identity. Thus, roots plus goals equals worth, and from this self-worth identity emerges.'[5]

Helping them to build a sense of identity

Over the years our children gradually build up a picture of who they are: 'I'm good at . . . I like . . . I feel . . . I have . . . I can . . . I belong . . . I know . . . That's me!' We want this picture to be both realistic and positive.

The young child's growing identity

We can interpret our children to themselves while they are very young, and many of us probably do this almost unconsciously in little asides and comments such as (I leave the situations to your imaginations and assume that the appropriate support and sympathy will have been given first):

- 'You're feeling cross because . . .'
- 'You're not well. That's why you feel hot all over and sad.'
- 'You feel good because . . .'
- 'You managed that well. You're good at . . .'
- 'You're not finding that easy because . . .'
- 'I know you like . . .'

We also help them to understand themselves by giving them choices to make, allowing them to try things on their own – whether this leads to success or failure – and trusting them with responsibility.

The adolescent's search for identity

Primary and junior children discover things about themselves almost haphazardly, but from puberty onwards things

5. Evelyn Peterson, *Who Cares?* (Paternoster).

change and the search for identity becomes very serious indeed and is linked with inner turmoil and physical, emotional and intellectual changes.

In answer to the young person's question, 'Who am I?' his family, friends, society, the media, and others, will give different answers. We want him to select the most truthful and positive ones. How can we do this? I think prayer, guidance and freedom are key words here.

Prayer

'Hold on to your teenager in prayer and bring him daily to God for him to work in your child's life. This is the time to talk to God about your child more than talking about God to your child.'[6] This is wise advice, and the prayer that we could do well to persist in is that our children will come to grasp the spiritual truth that to be truly and uniquely themselves, they need to be freely and wholly God's (see John 8:36).

Freedom and guidance

We must give our children room to be private, to discuss, question and experiment, while influencing them towards the best and highest.

Freedom from slavish imitation of their peers

Maturity involves being willing to reject the lumpy gruel of one's peers and one's parents. (Derek and Joan)

Encourage resistance to the jelly mould. (Dawn)

6. Anne Townsend, *Time for Change* (Marshall).

We felt we had to be a little tough with one of our children because she showed signs of being a slavish follower of others with no ideas of her own. So we refused to grant any wish that stemmed *solely* from what someone else did or had. In this way we tried to make her think out her reasons for wanting something without reference to anyone else. (Di)

In trying to find out who they are, children will experiment, particularly during adolescence, in all sorts of areas, including language, friendship, appearance, behaviour, fashion, hobbies and interests. We can help them by encouraging calm discussion on these and any other topics (see also pages 65 and 124).

Freedom from parental preconceptions and moulds

It's not only from their peers that our children need to be set free – but also from us, their parents. We must be very sure that we do not live for our children, or see them either as extensions of ourselves, obliged to fulfil our thwarted ambitions, 'do us proud' or 'be a credit to us', or as insurance against loneliness and old age. Such attitudes are selfish and may put pressures on our children which they are unable to bear. We must set them free to be themselves, not replicas of us and not forced to fit in with our expectations or ambitions. The same principle should apply in matters of faith. We want them to be Christians, but ultimately they must be free to reject or accept Christ, and in the mean time we would be wise to allow considerable freedom where our *preferences*, rather than *principles*, are concerned. If they choose to worship in a different way or place – let's just rejoice that they are worshipping the same God, and that he deals with each of us as individuals. It's exciting that we can learn from them as well as vice versa (Matt. 18:3).

STABILITY AND FLEXIBILITY

Having a flexible attitude is not the same as being a fickle, changeable person. It means being willing to adapt when it becomes clear that this is right or necessary, and this attitude is more likely to be found in stable, secure personalities.

Small babies need a routine and we should work one out as soon as possible, because it builds up their sense of security. But routines do not have to become invariable, and we can gradually accustom our little ones to changes. From time to time we can do things differently and, if our manner is confident and positive, the new pattern will be accepted and enjoyed.

Some children love routine and don't find it easy to think flexibly. I think it's helpful to encourage them to be brave and branch out now and again.

One of our children tends to be a bit of a ritualist and to assume that if we allow something one Monday, it will happen every subsequent Monday, world without end. So we have to think harder about saying 'Yes,' when she asks to do something, and sometimes when we do say it, we add, 'But that doesn't mean you can *always* have three chocolate biscuits on a Friday' (or whatever). (Di)

The combination of stability and flexibility is very important when our children reach adolescence. At this time they will be pushing against all authority figures, including parents. It's a physical fact that shoving hard against something that gives way easily isn't conducive to developing muscles and doesn't feel very satisfying either. Similarly, our children need something solid to react against and test.

At the same time, there will be many areas in which we will be freely admitting, 'I don't know it all. I've so much to learn. I haven't the answer.'

This model of firmness and flexibility, certainty and teachability is a good one for our children to copy. These qualities are needed in the material world where situations can change so rapidly (witness the employment situation). They are also vital in the spiritual realm, because God is a God of movement, and we need to be open to his direction: he always has more to teach us and more to do in us and through us.

CARE AND PROVISION

Survival needs include protection, food, clothing, sleep, shelter and exercise. We have to provide all these for our children at first, but gradually they learn to meet their own basic needs. Other things they need in order to develop as fully as possible have been discussed already.

If we do everything we can to meet all their needs generously, they will feel satisfied, valued and grateful. But from the time they can distinguish between needs and wishes, we will be teaching them that they can't have everything they want. For example, a child may want a fourth chocolate biscuit, but we may say 'No,' for one of several valid reasons: because we feel three is enough, or because letting him have it would be encouraging greed or lack of self-control, or because someone else wants it. If parents are generous and enjoy giving to their children when they can and think that it's right, they needn't feel in the least guilty when they have to say 'No'. We must get rid of the notion that not giving our children everything they want is a form of deprivation. Denying our child something for a good reason is an act of love and helping him to accept it with a good grace is part of training him for life – human and spiritual – since God meets our needs but does not necessarily supply our wants, and we have to trust that either way, he loves us.

The roots of confidence

We have been looking at thirteen ways in which a child could

97

be helped to face life confidently. Some of them are shown in the diagram on page 156. As you will see there, and from what has been said, Christian parents should be more effective than others in this area: we can not only root our children's worth in our opinion, but also, more importantly, in God's. A person who places his confidence in things or even in people – their love, praise or good opinion – might suddenly, like Job, lose all that. But even if he didn't, and his confidence survived this life, the moment he faced God he would realise his optimism had all been false. We want our children to have the confidence which comes from facing up to the way God sees us. In his sight we are equally worthless because 'all have sinned' and equally worthwhile because 'Christ died for all'. Therefore if we accept Jesus and all he has done for us, we can have the incomparable status, security and confidence which comes from being children of God, servants of Christ and 'temples' of the Holy Spirit.

5.

Facing life lovingly

Love the Lord your God with all your heart and with all your soul and with all your mind and with all your strength . . . Love your neighbour as yourself. (Mark 12:30,31).

'Love is like a butterfly,' says a popular song, to which I always want to retort, 'Some butterfly!' The fragile beauty of a butterfly provides a poor simile for true love – God's sort – which is essentially tough though not hard, sensitive though not sentimental or squeamish, comforting but not necessarily comfortable; soft without being easy-going. It washes dirty socks and feet but will not be anyone's door-mat – not through pride, but because using people is bad for the user. Its versatility is amazing: its eyes can be starry while its hands are wiping runny noses and bloody knees. Its demands are total, which is perhaps why there's not very much of it about.

We have already mentioned some ways in which our children can experience and start forming deep loving relationships with their Heavenly Father, family, and friends (see pages 59 to 65). But God's kind of love also includes consideration and service, so how can we show and encourage those?

CONSIDERATION

Each of you should look not only to your own interests, but also to the interests of others. (Phil. 2:4).

As always, children need to experience consideration if they are to know what it feels like and to show it to others.

How considerate are we to our families?

Hugh writes with great honesty:

> I have to be calm and sympathetic all day with patients and students, and I don't want to *have* to be the same when I get home. I, too, sometimes want to yell or withdraw.

I'm sure all those in professions where personal qualities are stretched to the full in the course of their work, as well as the natural givers and carers among us, would echo those feelings. Many of these people have a tendency to be wonderful to strangers and neighbours but hard on their own families, either because they have been giving out all day and can't make the effort any longer, or because they are inclined to be hard on themselves and to treat their nearest and dearest as extensions of themselves.

Surely there's something not quite right, in terms of balance and lifestyle, in these all-too-common situations:

- doctors caring for the health of hundreds but neglecting their own or their families'
- teachers neglecting the teaching needs of their own children while working hard on other people's
- pastors and counsellors giving hours of listening and counselling to the neighbourhood's youth, while giving very little time to their own?

Shouldn't consideration, like charity, begin at home, so that our children have an example to follow? If our teenagers shouldn't inflict their moods on us all the time, neither should we be so worn out that we rarely manage to give our family the sort of care, courtesy and expertise that we lavish on others daily.

How considerate are we to others?

How do we react to callers, visitors and people we meet as we go about our day-to-day lives? Children quickly notice whether or not we respond considerately to those who telephone or come with some need. They will observe, for instance, whether or not we switch off the television and put aside whatever we were doing in order to make visitors feel welcome.

Being real with people

While making an effort to welcome people, we needn't put on a front. Switching on a special brand of smile or bursting into breezy chat when visitors come, or spring cleaning the house and family in readiness for their arrival, might imply to our children that we, they and the home are just not good enough: pretence and cover-ups are needed. So we have to steer a middle course between not taking any trouble for people and putting on a show for them. The main thing is to be genuine with people and let them accept or reject us as we are.

Encouraging young children to be considerate

Small children are delightfully self-centred, but from toddlerhood onwards they are able to distinguish more and more clearly between themselves and others. Therefore it's quite reasonable to restrain them from kicking, biting and hitting people, and point out that while they might be enjoying the proceedings, those on the receiving end are not! Similarly if a mum has a headache and her child is being noisy, it's perfectly reasonable for her to ask him to be quieter and explain why. This will introduce the idea that it's good to stop doing things – even those we enjoy – when we see they are upsetting someone else.

Sharing, taking turns and good manners are also best taught in the context of consideration for others. For example, it's better to say, 'If you chew with your mouth open, the person opposite can see all your half-chewed food,' than, 'Nice children keep their mouths closed when they are eating.'

Encouraging older children to be considerate

It's hard for adolescents to think of others, because their own feelings are so all-consuming as they ricochet from soaring optimism through rage and frustration to depression. At the same time, it's not right that the whole house should shake and reverberate all the time as a result of their moods or music. So what can we do?

I think again we have to steer a middle course – between being 'underwhelmed' and overwhelmed by our adolescents' moods and feelings. If we ignore or dismiss them completely and give pat answers to their doubts, they will conclude that we neither care nor understand. But if we take their feelings too much to heart, we won't be any help to them at all. Indeed, if our children can see that their feelings of anger and depression, for instance, can trigger off the same feelings in us, they could start feeling insecure and guilty on top of everything else!

So we have to show them that we care, and are prepared to listen and understand, but encourage them to think of others too, perhaps sometimes by pointed remarks such as:

- 'It's not fair to inflict your moods on the whole family.'
- 'You feel angry – is that a good enough reason for snapping everybody's head off?'
- 'Please go up to your room until you can sort out your feelings and let me know if there's anything I can do to help.'

This could be combined with much praise and encouragement for every single effort they make to control themselves out of consideration for others, and with teaching about God's considerate, compassionate love for us (Ps. 104:13,14).

But I stress again, we do have to put our lives where our mouths are in this matter! Are teenagers the only ones who inflict their moods on the rest of the family? Like it or not, mothers seem to influence the atmosphere in the home more than anyone else, so we need to watch our moods. Often, in thinking back over a scene, I realise that some remark or attitude of mine triggered it off.

SERVICE

I am among you as one who serves. (Luke 22:27).
You also should wash one another's feet. (John 13:14).

These verses go beyond considering others to actively serving them in a spirit of humility and self-denial. This is a very mature attitude but we can begin encouraging it in a small way while our children are young.

Serving each other in the home

Although parents will carry the workload, I'm sure they should not do all the giving while the children do all the taking. Encouraging and valuing our children's contributions from an early age can prepare the way for the idea of mutual serving.

Often small children want to please so it's not hard to involve them. Cooking, cleaning, tidying, sorting, washing, planting, raking, picking fruit and many other jobs round the house and garden can be cut down to child-size.

Under-fives will accept *anything* as fun, provided the parents are enthusiastic about it and treat it as fun. (Rebecca)

It isn't possible to make everything fun all the time, but children can gain a different sort of enjoyment from doing things for people and receiving their thanks and appreciation for it. Helping to clear up, particularly their own mess and untidiness, making their own beds, putting their dirty clothes in the wash – are wonderfully helpful ways in which children can serve their parents, as well as excellent training in responsibility.

It grieves and astonishes me when I hear of parents doing all sorts of jobs which it would be more appropriate for their children to be doing for themselves. Mothers are particularly prone to wait on their sons in this way, thus probably making a rod for the backs of their sons' future wives, among other things!

Using our homes to serve others

I'm sure Christian homes and families can be beacons of light and havens of stability and comfort for all sorts of people. Are we welcoming into our homes only like-minded and similarly-placed friends or are we including:
- families where there is unemployment
- single parents and their families
- newcomers to the church or district
- immigrants
- students in bed-sits or halls of residence
- children from nearby boarding schools
- our children's Sunday School teachers or youth leaders, so that they don't have to cook as well as teach on Sunday mornings
- single people and others living alone, e.g. widows, widowers
- ex-prisoners
- people recovering from breakdowns and living in 'half-way houses' or institutions
- old people

- families with a sick or handicapped member in them
- children of missionaries while their parents are abroad?

Of course we have to balance the needs and wishes of these people against the needs and wishes of our own families, but asking them to make occasional sacrifices, e.g. missing television programmes because of having guests in for an evening meal, is not unreasonable and makes our priorities clear to them.

Links with the needy in other places

Looking farther afield, are we linked as a family either directly or through the church to the needy and those organisations seeking to help them? Do we have links with (support, pray for, exchange news with, give to) any of the following:
- a missionary family/mission (home and abroad)
- a third world child/family
- a local or national group engaged in helping the needy or trying to promote Christian standards in our own country
- someone in prison for Christ or an organisation working for such people
- an international aid or relief organisation?

The spirit of our giving and sharing is very important. We need to see and teach it not as a duty only but as a blessing and something very exciting to do. If giving is done out of love for and with the love of Jesus – and therefore sensitively, humbly and willingly – it can be sheer joy.

6.

Facing life courageously

Suffering produces perseverance; perseverance, character; and character, hope. (Rom. 5:3,4).

Facing life courageously ourselves and helping our children to do the same is absolutely vital, since life is fraught with difficulties. Children do not have to be very old before they experience them: they cannot manage to tie up their shoelaces, the child at playgroup keeps hitting them, they can't seem to learn to read, the other children are calling them names, their teacher doesn't like them . . .

Early morning tummies and science headaches

We have just had a period of early morning tummy aches. I find it hard to send my child to school in tears, but his teacher assures me he's fine once he's settled. The underlying cause seems to be that his best friend has moved from one class to another. I feel that if I give in just once, he will 'use' this in future. I always tell him that his teacher will phone me if he doesn't feel better later. (Penny)

One of our sons said to us, 'Do you remember when I used to get science headaches?' When I seemed puzzled, he said, 'Didn't you notice that I always managed to make myself sick when science happened?' A very fierce, insensitive master was responsible for this. (Deborah)

A school resister

My child walked every step to school backward. It was psychological warfare at its very worst. He hid his socks under the mattress – anywhere. By the time he was six, he could spend thirty minutes non-stop giving me ten good reasons why he shouldn't go to school and the harmful effect it was having on him.

He was an only child and we felt that it was right to send him to boarding school at the age of eight. Now at eighteen he is grateful, but the moral blackmail to remove him from school at each minor crisis was intense. He survived and got educated. I got grey hair and wrinkles.

Love is kind but never soft. Children must grow up with some kind of backbone, because life is hard and there are bound to be some rough patches. (Dawn)

Separation – through the parents' work

It was a traumatic experience letting go of a twelve-year-old to be educated eight thousand miles away. I sobbed my way through the days after the airport farewell until one day I said broken-heartedly to an older Christian, 'I find it so hard to give up the rights to motherhood.'

'What rights?' she asked. This was the beginning of an understanding of a rather devastating little area of knowledge which had escaped my attention up till that time. The child wasn't mine: he was God's. I only had him on trust for a few short years. The message to me at that time was, 'Hands off.'

In Old Testament times, Joseph and David went through trials which God allowed them to experience for the sake of the finished product but from which their parents would surely have protected them, if they could have. I began to see this and apply it to our situation. I could so easily have been the over-protective parent, sheltering our son from winds that God meant to blow on him for the sake of the finished product. (Hazel)

For parents who are inclined to be over-protective of or over-dependent on their children, such objectivity and trust in God are essential. Being objective is not the same as being detached or uncaring. It's an attitude that enables us to see what is right and necessary *for the child*, despite our feelings in the matter.

Bullying

Most children will experience some form of verbal or physical bullying in their lives. A sixteen-year-old lad told me that he thought the verbal sort was far, far worse than the other – thus giving the lie to the ridiculous playground jingle that 'sticks and stones may break your bones, but words can never hurt you'.

Children most at risk are usually those who stand out as different in character or appearance – the solitary, big-eared, long-nosed, under-sized, over-sized, nervous, weak, slow, handicapped or very bright child.

All our children suffered from bullying to a greater or lesser degree and the more I talk to parents, the more I am convinced about just how common this problem is. I notice that Mountbatten was bullied for years in his teens – but perhaps this experience was part of the making of him.

Our eldest daughter, Kate, came in for a fair bit of verbal bullying from one friend, Natalie, whose clothes were always much better than hers. As Kate was very clothes-conscious, this really got her down. I asked her what her other friend, Sylvia, did when Natalie teased her and she replied, 'She just laughs, so Natalie doesn't bother with her.' A bit later, Natalie came to school wearing yet another new school skirt and said to Kate, 'You've only got one, haven't you?' and Kate replied, 'So what! We have other things to spend our money on.' When I heard about this, I was pleased because I felt Kate was learning to cope.

Someone I worked with said that when her son was bullied, she told him, 'If you don't go back and give them as good as you got, I shall give you even worse later on.' Needless to say, she wasn't a Christian, but isn't there something in what she said? And her method worked!

I was bullied at one school. My parents used to plead with me to stand up to the bullies, but I never would because of the verse about loving one's enemies. With hindsight, I realise I used this as an excuse for not facing up to the problem.

When I left school and started nursing, I had to face aggressive people again and went under until, during my last year of training, I realised that there was a way of standing up to aggressors without being rude. When I returned to nursing years later, I was very timid once more, but after about a year of misery under an impatient ward sister, I came reluctantly to the conclusion that it was people like me who gave the impression that Christianity was a chicken-hearted way of life. It took a tremendous effort of will and prayer for me to snap out of my timid ways, but when I did, I got on well with the ward sister. There is a lot of very bad nursing in this hospital, so I need to be firm in order to stand up for patients' rights.

From my own experiences and those of our children, I would say that:

- if a bullied child cries and pleads for mercy it only makes matters worse
- taking a child away from the place where the bullying

happens may give him a much-needed breathing space, but it doesn't solve the problem he will certainly have to face again some time

- it's possible for the bullied child to stand up to his aggressors without being vicious, spiteful or wrong (Is it really unchristian for a boy to knock down another in fair fight or for a girl to answer back when she is attacked verbally?)

- Jesus said, 'Do not resist an evil person. If someone strikes you on the right cheek, turn to him the other also' (Matt. 5:39) – but he stood up to and denounced his enemies, the Pharisees (Matt. 23:29,33). So evidently there is a time and place for submitting and a time and place for resisting. Also, we need to see *how* Jesus submitted. When facing a totally unfair trial and then enduring death, he displayed neither haughtiness nor cringing misery, but was silent and dignified. Throughout his life he managed to hold in balance the acceptance of injury and humiliation, and a firm rebuttal of evil. (Lisa)

Guidelines

Parents suffer a great deal as they see their children going through difficulties. How can we react wisely and lovingly in these situations? Should we fight their battles for them, remove them from the battlefield, or do nothing?

I think there are times when it's right for parents to intervene. For example, it's now possible to do something about very protruding teeth, noses and ears (though in the matter of teeth, I do wonder whether the contraptions some children have to wear do more psychological damage than the fault they are correcting!). So if these are causing our children a great deal of misery, it seems compassionate to have something done about them.

Similarly, it might be right to remove a child from a school or class where he is very unhappy, or to intervene in some other direct way.

But more often than not it's better to put our efforts into enabling the child to cope successfully with the situation. We could help him by suggesting what he might say or do to avoid future trouble or improve a situation; by assuring him that God cares and that we will be praying for him all the time; and by praising him for any efforts on his part.

If our children do learn to face and overcome difficulties through our encouragement and in the strength God gives, it will help them to grow in faith, confidence, endurance and sympathy. These are very necessary qualities for Christians who not only have to face all the usual problems, but are also engaged in spiritual war.

Human courage is not enough in spiritual war, so our children also need to develop spiritual courage, which comes from:

- knowing we are weak but God is strong
- depending on God and trusting that he's there
- knowing we are where he wants us to be in the battle
- knowing Jesus has already defeated the world, the flesh and the devil
- knowing we are wearing spiritual armour (Eph. 6:10–17).

While not wanting to over-emphasise the activity of Satan in the world and in our lives, we do need gradually to make our children aware of this. During adolescence, they will usually show a great interest in such matters. This will extend to the occult and other aspects of the supernatural, other religions and the sects. So we need to inform them of the biblical principles on all these matters, and pray very hard that they will not become involved – the fascination with secret societies which promise knowledge, love or power can be very strong. We want our young people to be aware of the powers of evil but not obsessed by them – and ready to engage in spiritual war against them in God's strength and courage.

But it isn't only in these ways that Satan shows his hand.

No matter what school – or even pre-school group – our children go to, they will come across others who lie, cheat, steal and are rude to the teachers, and they will either react very indignantly or start imitating such behaviour. We must understand just how hard it is for children to cope with one set of standards at home and another at school, while reinforcing what is right.

7.

Facing life honestly and hopefully

There is no one who does good, not even one. (Rom. 3:12).
God made him who had no sin to be sin for us, so that in him we might become the righteousness of God. (2 Cor. 5:21).
You . . . are God's temple . . . All things are yours. (1 Cor. 3:16,21).
We . . . are being transformed into his likeness with ever-increasing glory. (2 Cor. 3:18).

Bringing up children to see life with God as crucial and central is really helping them to face facts honestly but remain hopeful. Christians can be both realistic and idealistic.

GOOD AND EVIL

We will need to spell out very clearly what evil is and explode some popular myths about it. Evil is whatever displeases God. We can no longer assume that all children will be taught God's standards outside the home. On the contrary, they are likely to come across children and adults in real life and in books and plays who flout any or all of the Ten Commandments. It's considered rather smart to cheat the government of some of its taxes, 'nick' things from a shop, or even from one's parents, or acquire them through their having 'fallen off the back of a lorry'. Our children's popstar or film star heroes could well lie, cheat and steal with charm and impunity.

Our children need to hear loud and clear from us:

- the biblical standards of wrong and right
- that evil is inherent in all of us and in every part of our being
- that there is an evil personality behind all the sin in the world and he is God's and our enemy
- that evil is spoiling creation and people's lives and cuts us off from God.

When our children are young we should, I think, concentrate on teaching and showing them right and wrong. Some people shrink from giving rules to their children, but these are exactly right for our young ones. They cannot handle long explanations and abstract reasoning, but they can grasp, 'Don't do this – it's wrong,' or, 'Do do that – it's right.' Knowing the rules and limits is part of a child's security and if we love and understand him, we must not shrink from spelling them out.

As they grow into adolescence and see the sin within and around, we can teach them more about the source and effects of evil.

Alongside this gloomy picture, we can give our children the biblical standards of goodness and keep holding up to them and encouraging them to discern what is true, noble, right, pure, lovely, admirable, excellent and praiseworthy (Phil. 4:8). Above all, we will want to point them to Jesus. He made goodness so *attractive*! Our young people are being told in all sorts of ways – through TV commercials for example – that it's boring to be good and exciting to be naughty. So it's very important that we should try to disabuse them of this notion and to demonstrate an exciting, attractive goodness, thus proving: 'How monotonously alike all the great tyrants and conquerors have been: how gloriously different are the saints.'[1]

Our children also need to be taught that:
- Jesus died so we could be forgiven and given God's goodness as a gift

1. C. S. Lewis, *Mere Christianity* (Collins).

- the Holy Spirit, as we trust and obey Jesus, keeps on making us more like Jesus.

FORGIVENESS

Only if the Christian doctrine of forgiveness is understood and practised, can life be faced hopefully, so this needs to be taught and lived out between all the members of Christian families.

We insist on saying sorry. We feel this is an essential ingredient in getting on with people. 'Sorry' can solve a great many problems, but is hard to say. If a child has been brought up to say it, it's a great help.

Ray, my husband, didn't start saying sorry till we'd been married a couple of years, but when he did, it made all the difference. His family had always let things blow over instead of getting them cleared away. (Rebecca)

To say sorry in our family was regarded as a total loss of face, in that one was admitting to a fault. My mother had, and still has, a colossal inferiority complex and I think this has rubbed off on us. (Ray)

Some might argue that making a child say sorry when he doesn't feel it, is teaching him to be insincere. But sorry can be seen as an admission that one has done wrong, not as a statement about how one feels. Also, so often we have to do right and wait for the feelings to follow. When we say sorry, the reaction of love and forgiveness from the other person is likely to produce truly 'sorry' feelings even if they were absent before.

As well as saying sorry to one another, parents and children need to humble themselves constantly before God and ask his forgiveness. We need to teach that God only wants us to do this in order to be able to forgive us, lift us up and send us on our way with his joy and peace inside us (see also page 140).

SUFFERING AND DEATH

As loving parents, we will do our best to protect our children from unnecessary, overwhelming suffering. But when we cannot or should not so protect them, we will love them in and support them through their pain or hardship. On the basis of these experiences, and of our own reactions to suffering, we can teach them that God allows suffering in this world, and no one is exempt from it – not even Jesus was; he loves and supports us in our pain, is in control, can bring good out of it and will one day wipe every tear from our eyes (Rev. 21:4).

The subject of death can be approached with the same realism and idealism. It is inevitable, it comes sometimes in painful ways and it is sad for loved ones; but for the Christian who has passed from spiritual death to spiritual life, physical death is simply a door into God's presence where there are joy and eternal pleasures (Ps. 16:11).

When our children experience the death of a pet or a loved one, the best we can do is to encourage them to express their grief to us and to God. In comforting them, we can tell them that God is a comforter and longs to comfort them too (2 Cor. 1:3,4). As we teach them about heaven, all sorts of questions will be asked, e.g. 'Will my pet hamster go to heaven?' I leave you to sort out your answers to questions like that! All we can say with certainty is that God is fair and loving and has promised that all his children will one day live in his home with him for ever.

PEOPLE

Even young children can be helped to develop positive

attitudes to people. Parental example is important here, and also a child's attitude to himself (see page 92ff).

With greater maturity, our young people can be helped to see people both more realistically and more hopefully. They can see them (and themselves) as they really are, while being confident of the transformation which could be effected (Rom. 12:2).

8.

Facing life discerningly

So we fix our eyes not on what is seen, but on what is unseen. For what is seen is temporary, but what is unseen is eternal. (2 Cor. 4:18).
The things that come from the Spirit of God . . . are spiritually discerned. The spiritual man makes judgments about all things. (1 Cor. 2:14,15).

Being a Christian should involve us in making value judgments about everything in life. We need to learn to see people, possessions, the world about us, behaviour, daily life – *everything* – with a Christian mind.

A RIGHT ATTITUDE TO EVENTS

This can be fostered very naturally within the Christian family. It can become the practice for the family to talk and pray about things that have happened or are about to happen. Whether these events are sad or happy, the parents' attitude and words can teach the children that God is behind them, that he shares our joy or sorrow in them, and that he can bring good out of anything if we keep trusting, praising and obeying him. When something sad happens, to say, 'I trust you to bring some good out of this, Lord,' rather than, 'Why me, Lord?' requires a good deal of spiritual maturity, but we can lay the foundations for just that attitude.

A RIGHT ATTITUDE TO THINGS

In word, deed and attitude, we can convey very early to our children the message that possessions are gifts from a loving God. They are to be received gratefully, looked after and used properly, enjoyed and shared generously, but never hoarded or prized above the Giver, or above people and relationships.

Or we can convey a different message. How upset are we when things are not just so in our homes? Can we wait patiently for new things or even do without? If a child accidentally breaks something, do we treat it as a major tragedy? Our children will certainly notice what we do and say in such situations and draw their own conclusions from it.

The toddler and his houseproud mother

If parents haven't sorted out their priorities earlier, they will certainly have to do so when their children reach the toddler stage. A houseproud, perfectionist mother will then discover that her wishes are definitely at variance with those of her pint-sized vandals! *They* want to explore everything, everywhere, all the time; *she* wants an immaculate house. So she must ask herself, 'What's the priority here – my toddler's need to explore and experiment, or my need to have a beautiful, spotless house?'

For the Christian mother there can be only one answer. This will entail rearranging her priorities and accepting less-than-perfect standards for the time being in the relatively unimportant area of possessions. When the children have grown and flown – all too quickly – she will probably have years in which to polish her furniture, but she can never recall the time when her God-given task was her child's welfare.

There may be some women outside television commercials

who manage to combine dream homes with thriving toddlers on an average income, but most of us in this imperfect world have to opt for *either* house beautiful *or* happy small children.

This does not mean that our toddler should be allowed to do exactly as he pleases! But do let's be as generous a possible in what we allow, remembering that God, the perfect Parent, only prohibited the use of *one* tree among hundreds of others to be freely enjoyed!

Some parents choose to give their small children almost total freedom in a childproofed room. The disadvantage of this becomes obvious when such a child is taken into other people's non-childproofed homes. His parents cannot relax for an instant, since he has been led to believe that the rule about things is – if you can reach them, you can kick them bite them or hurl them across the room!

Others think it's best to give the child the freedom of the house, while taking time to teach and train him to handle things properly. The disadvantage of this could be that because of this necessary teaching and training, 'things' may assume a greater importance than perhaps they should at such a formative time of life.

Probably a combination of the two ideas is best – giving the child a play area that isn't completely childproofed but doesn't contain too many forbidden objects. When he has learnt to play safely and sensibly within those limits, he could be allowed more space and more playthings.

Cutting down on things?

Many Christians are being made to think seriously about simplifying their lifestyle, and cutting down on possessions is one way of moving towards this. Through the media, we are now being made aware more than ever before of the millions of poor, homeless, hungry and unemployed people there are in the world. Various Christian writers have urged us in different ways to 'live more simply so that others may simply live'.

So we have to ask ourselves: Are we too cluttered up by things? Should our lifestyle, including our entertaining, be plainer and more economical?

John Taylor feels that Christians should call a halt when they have 'enough', and suggests that each family could begin a 'joyful resistance movement' for which two of the slogans might be, 'The price tag is too high,' and 'You can't take it with you.'

I think our teenagers are far more likely to be influenced by this sort of approach than by long, serious sermons.

To summarise

A discerning attitude to things means looking after them well and sharing them because they are God's gifts, but giving them a low priority in relation to people: things were made for people, not vice versa. Our homes should be neither slums nor show-pieces, neither completely chaotic nor fanatically tidy. My heart warms to John Taylor's concept of: '. . . a kind of bareness, a kind of shabbiness even, which is beautiful because it speaks of beautiful priorities, and all who share the same priorities feel at home in it.'[1]

Discerning the crucial issues

Another way in which parents can show discernment and balanced judgment to their children is by distinguishing clearly between what is really important and what is not, and making an issue only of the former.

Make a great stand on hair length or nail varnish and you

1. John V. Taylor, *Enough is Enough* (SCM Press).

may find you have no steam left for tackling sleeping around and alcohol. (Betty)

To these one could add – drugs, the occult, shop-lifting, vandalism, glue-sniffing, and others. We must be solidly against these and other dangerous, degrading and unbiblical practices.

But what about the other things that loom large at different times in our children's lives: television, parties, pop, clothes and their heroes or idols? How are we to show and teach discernment in these areas?

Television

What attitude should Christian parents take to this box which, we are told, some children will have watched for a total of eight years by the time they reach twenty-one? *More bad than good and therefore ban the set?* Rebecca and Ray who had a television for a time and then sent it back, feel that:

- historic events, nature and travel programmes, and sport were very good
- children's programmes were mixed and some cartoons definitely induced nightmares in imaginative children
- one so-called realistic portrayal of life at a school was a disgraceful suggester of rudeness, shoplifting and rebellion
- adult programmes were often ruined by the kind of language, humour and sexual scenes one would not wish to view in the presence of godly adults
- true even-handed news reporting was comparatively rare; instead there was a tendency to report the sensational and to represent everything as confrontation 'win-or-lose' situations – very unhelpful for those working in national, international, industrial or any other sort of relations
- TV can be a powerful form of auto-suggestion – the more

so as it is bought by the parents and installed in the home

- TV can, at a subtle level, erode Christian standards through bad language, blasphemous exclamations, casual sex, jokes about 'bedding' others, violence, disrespect, rudeness, 'beautiful' plays looking 'seriously' at sexual deviations, etc.
- TV can cut down on communication between members of a family, produce anti-social attitudes to friends and visitors, be a source of contention, and act like a drug on some people, producing dependency and loss of will power
- without television, more time is available for hobbies and reading, and there can be more scope for the imagination.

This couple expresses a view that many Christians have. Others feel that it's better to have a television but be selective.

Limit hours and programmes and encourage discrimination? This is definitely not an easy option. It requires self-control, tact and a strong will. It may also mean that parents have to watch more television than they want to, in order to be able to discuss the programmes with their children.

Possible guidelines. Parents have to decide what they are happy for their children to watch on their own, what they will ban and what they will allow and discuss.

We try to distinguish between 'trivial rubbish' and 'dangerous rubbish' and allow a little of the former and none of the latter – but we flounder a lot, I'm sure. In the 'harmful' category, we would want to put plays and films showing sexual perversion, gratuitous violence and horror.

We are also not too happy about programmes in children's viewing time based on non-Christian religions such as Buddhism and Eastern mystical thought. Children who do not know the main tenets of these religions could be unduly influenced by the appealing way they are portrayed. The answer could be to stop them watching such programmes or to take time to inform them about the religions concerned.

Children most at risk. Some children do 'grow out of' television. These are usually those who by nature or through maturity are strong-willed and discriminating. Such children, given the right guidelines and a good relationship with their parents, will watch television selectively – if at all – in the end.

But a child who is, by nature or through lack of maturity, passive, easily-led and not able to make critical judgments, will need tighter controls, active encouragement to develop alternative and more creative and demanding interests than TV watching, and training in self-control and discrimination.

Discussing programmes critically. Opening a discussion by dismissing as 'utter rubbish' something our children have enjoyed will probably alienate them. What we want to create is an atmosphere of calm objectivity so that a programme can be discussed through questions such as:

- did it show ordinary people or a few 'odd balls'?
- were they portrayed realistically or not/at their best or worst?
- did it help you to understand or think about anything more clearly, or not?
- do you think the writer wanted to shock/amuse/inform – or what?
- how has it made you feel and are you glad you saw it?

Discussion is one way of helping our children to start sorting out the first-rate from the second-rate, the trivial from the deep, the good from the bad, the false from the true, the real from the phoney. Apropos of phoneyness, John Taylor suggests that the slogan, 'Who are you kidding?' . . . 'needs to be quoted with pride – best of all by a family in unison every time a television commercial appears on the screen. We must learn to treat with ribald laughter all those patently phoney demonstrations.'[2]

2. John V. Taylor, *Enough is Enough* (SCM Press).

Barbie writes:

> Help! How does one cope on a limited budget with a child
> who wants to be in the fashion, like all her friends?

It's quite a problem – this business of being sympathetic
to our child's wishes, while trying to encourage him to get his
priorities right.

One thing is clear. It's bad stewardship to be wasteful, so
we probably won't feel it's right to buy new clothes unless
they are needed, except at Christmas or for birthdays.

Also, what we buy must be right for the family's finances,
adequate for the purpose for which they were designed, and
suitable for the child concerned. For example, we wouldn't
want to buy shoes which would damage our child's feet, no
matter how much he wanted them.

However, with those provisos, we could surely go some
way towards satisfying his desire for fashionable clothes. If
money is a problem, perhaps we could forgo something we
enjoy – e.g. a meal out, a visit to the theatre or a sporting
activity – so as to be able to afford something he really wants.
This would show him clearly that we do care, and are
prepared to make sacrifices.

At the same time, we will be wanting to encourage him to
form and make personal judgments – and not do things
simply because other people do them. If the priorities in our
homes are right, this will help him to develop true perspectives for himself. Once again, we need to be honest about our
motives.

Be very sure you are not worried about 'losing face'
yourself because of what your children are or do. If you are
concerned about your own reputation because of them,
they will despise you. (Betty)

As the children grew up, we were asked all the usual questions, e.g. 'Can I go to a disco?' The answer was 'No,' when they first started asking at the age of eleven. By the age of fourteen they were allowed to go but under strict limitations, e.g. being met by father at 10 p.m.

We usually said 'No,' to Sunday parties. If we said 'Yes,' we always said what time we would collect them, regardless of whether the party was just getting going at that time or not. We didn't leave it to anyone else to bring them home until they were much older.

When the children were older and wanted to go to parties, we would ask, 'Will the parents be at home? Will there be drinks? What sort of people are they? Do you think you will be happy there?' Sometimes the child would then decide to refuse the invitation.

I have always thanked God that our children were not influenced by friends who took drugs, drank a lot, had free views about pre-marital sex, stole money, were vandals, dabbled with the occult, or engaged in other unhelpful adolescent pursuits. Therefore our children were not exposed to these temptations until they left home at the age of eighteen. Unfortunately they did meet some of those temptations then and I think they must have been pretty hard hit by them. (Now they are grown up, and have told us some fairly hair-raising stories!) But when they left home, praise the Lord, they were strong enough as Christians and as people to withstand and, in some cases, help others to do the same. (Prue)

There shouldn't be a kill-joy attitude in us. Our children need to know that we want them to enjoy life and have fun with their friends. But when their idea of what having a good time involves clashes with ours, we have to judge the child and the situation and decide whether to say 'Yes,' with or without provisos, trusting him, or at least allowing him to learn from experience, or 'No,' while trying to persuade him that we have done so out of love.

Pop

Pop is one level of communication for a big percentage of teenagers. Can we deprive those who enjoy it of their 'heart language'? Christian entertainers who communicate in this language are a great help, and there are some around.

Many of today's songs are ballads which try to say something about life. Songs with doubtful lyrics could be talked over. We could point out gently that if one hears unsavoury lyrics over and over again in conducive settings one can be brain-washed to some extent. We could also encourage them to be critical of all that they read, listen to or watch, even if this means that they have to 'stand up and be counted'. Perhaps they could be persuaded to analyse the Top Thirty sometimes and this might help them to start being more critical and selective. (Hazel)

This strikes me as wise and compassionate advice. I would also suggest that it might be good to limit the actual *quantity* of music that a teenager listens to. If pop is one form of relaxation among others, its influence is likely to be less all-pervasive than if it's a permanent feature, albeit in the background, like wallpaper. However good it may be, it represents a fairly limited range of musical and literary styles.

Idols and heroes

When we were young, our idols were footballers, film-stars, or even preachers. But today it's mostly pop-stars. There is a natural hero-worshipping stage and we need to help our young folk to discern, in time, who are worthy heroes and who are not, and to spot what may be morally harmful in what their heroes do, say or sing. This puts an onus on us to keep in touch, albeit lightly, with what they are seeing and hearing. (Mary)

Keeping in touch but not getting too involved

I think the word 'lightly' is important here. We shouldn't overdo things and start trying to ape our young people. When I hear parents boasting that they and their teenagers could pass or have passed for sisters or brothers, I wonder whether the children concerned are as pleased as their mothers or fathers! According to this teenager, trendy parents are *not* what is needed.

> Our son once said to us, 'I'm glad you chug along, occasionally liking or tolerating some of the things I like, but I wouldn't want you to be all trendy, liking all pop music and so on, because then I'd have to be more "way out", just to be different.' (Di)

I think this gives us a clue about one quite important aspect of the much-discussed generation-gap. This gap occurs in part because young people need to force a little emotional distance between themselves and their parents, so that they are freer to experiment with a view to self-discovery.

In conclusion

Television, pop and pop-stars, fashion and parties, are just a few of the influences in our children's lives. Others are mentioned elsewhere. We want our children to enjoy whatever is good and helpful in all these areas, but not to be enslaved by them, or to accept everything uncritically. Moderation, good sense and good taste – these we can try to encourage and show, but it is the Holy Spirit who gives spiritual discernment which distinguishes not just the poor from the good, but the good from the best. So we must pray hard that he will do this, while creating a climate, through teaching and example, in which it is easy for him to work.

9.

Facing life responsibly

Freely you have received, freely give. (Matt. 10:8).
From everyone who has been given much, much will be demanded; and from the one who has been entrusted with much, much more will be asked. (Luke 12:48).

Facing life responsibly means taking responsibility for one's actions and choices – i.e. making decisions, seeing them through and taking the consequences – managing oneself and one's life well and using all God's other gifts properly.

DECISION-MAKING

The secret is to start small. Very young children may need to be helped by unthreatening and 'protected' questions such as: 'Which would you rather do/have/eat . . . *first?*' Later on a child might be able to cope with, 'Would you like to go to the park or the playground?' and not panic at the thought of what he is missing by choosing the one or the other. Later still, he might need the freedom of, 'What would you like to do?'

It's important not to give children too much choice too soon. I have seen little ones getting really distressed because they have been asked to make a decision which was simply beyond them.

As they grow older, they can have a bigger share of the decision-making concerning school subjects, exams, holidays and clubs.

TAKING THE CONSEQUENCES

It's very easy for parents to go on picking up the pieces for their children when it would be far better for everyone if they didn't. Rushing to school with a book they've forgotten to stop them getting into trouble could be just one example of being over-protective.

We can also wait on our children too much – being a taxi service, for instance, when they could quite easily walk or take a bus.

SEEING THINGS THROUGH

If we want our children to be 'faithful till death' to a marriage partner, we will probably need to start training them in 'stickability' early, since the message they will be receiving from most other sources will be, 'If you don't like it, give it up and try something else.' The 'it' in question may be a marriage, a career or a hobby. Unfaithfulness in all areas is rapidly becoming a cult.

How can we stop the rot as far as our children are concerned? Most importantly, we must show faithfulness in relation to our partner, our children, our friends and responsibilities. Then we can encourage our children to see things through to the end when they take on a job at home or school, join a club, start a course, and so on. Of course children need to experiment, but committing themselves to something one day and opting out the next is not conducive to learning anything – except a pattern of unfaithfulness!

SELF-CONTROL

A toddler in a temper tantrum is a toddler out of his own control. Three mothers share their experiences or suggestions on this matter.

Mandy lay kicking and screaming in the High Street. I tried to calm her but failed dismally, so stood back and waited for the storm to pass. Several women went by and berated me as 'cruel' and 'callous' and each time Mandy would raise her head a little and scream more loudly. After a while, she stopped, just like that, got up, trotted across, took my hand and said, 'Where are we going now, Mummy?' (Rebecca)

Instinctively I felt I should 'contain' a child in a rage. I held, comforted and encouraged through to the exhausted end. Years later I saw a film from Canada where seriously deprived children were treated in the same way, while those holding them repeated gently and lovingly, 'You can't hurt yourself. You're safe. You can't hurt us. You're all right.' (Deborah)

Hilary suggests what a mother might say to a small child in a tantrum. His reactions are left to our imaginations!

'It's no good your having a tantrum because it won't get you what you want.'
   'If you go on shouting, crying and stamping, I'm going to take you . . . (somewhere quiet) and I'm not going to listen to you till you've stopped.'
   'What was it you wanted?'
   'Will you ask me for it properly?' (If he does, give a reasonable answer and perhaps a small reward for calming down and asking properly, even though you may feel you must say 'No' to his request.)

Three different reactions – ignoring, holding and reasoning with the child – but in each case the mother remained calm and in control of the situation, however she might have been feeling inside. This is important.

What caused the tantrum?

Also important, is to know our child and try to understand why he behaved as he did. It may be very obvious: he wanted something, we said, 'Sorry, no,' and so he threw a tantrum. If this is the case, and we give him what he wanted for the sake of peace, we are giving him the wrong message. What he will be hearing is, 'Getting angry is a good way of getting what I want,' when what he *should* be hearing is, 'You will never get your own way through behaving like that.'

But the child may not have become angry through having his will thwarted. He may have reacted like that because he was too hungry and over-tired to cope any longer, or because he couldn't get our attention or make himself understood. Or perhaps he was over-stimulated and blew his top as a way of releasing pent-up, mixed up, powerful emotions.

When he has calmed down, especially if he was being too noisy for us to say anything to him before, it might be helpful to reduce the situation to size by a few calm words such as:

- 'I know you behaved like that because you were feeling tired and hungry (or whatever) and I'm sorry, so let's . . . but next time will you . . . ?'
- 'I do understand how badly you wanted that ice-cream/toy . . . but getting angry like that won't do you any good. Next time I say "No," and you feel like doing that again, I'm sure you'll remember that and manage much better and I'll be very pleased.'

By saying things like this we are staying in control while putting a little bit of the onus on to the child's shoulders.

If we come to the conclusion, however, that the tantrums are simply the child's way of letting off steam and expressing pent-up emotions, we might have to weather them as best we can, or see if more free outdoor play with lots of physical exercise will give him the release he needs.

Adolescent moods

The same basic principles apply when we are trying to keep teenage moods within reasonable bounds while encouraging self-control. It might be helpful to suggest that our adolescents could try writing down their feelings in prose or perhaps poetry. This could well prove a useful outlet, and help them to gain some self-knowledge as well as better control of themselves.

TIME-MANAGEMENT

The early morning scramble before school can be very fraught as doors slam, feet pound up and down stairs and cries of 'Where's my PE kit/ruler/shoe/dinner money . . . ?' ring out. Every morning we vow we'll keep calm and send off our children with a kiss, hug and prayer. But all too often by the time they leave, the atmosphere is so explosive that kisses, hugs and prayers are out of the question, and our children stomp off feeling strained and resentful, leaving us guilt-ridden or furious or both.

I think it's worth making an effort to bring some order into the early morning pattern. For a start, the children could be responsible for getting all their things ready the night before, and for remembering things like notes or money to be taken to school.

They could also be encouraged to draw up their own checklist. Anna has a five-finger plan to make sure she does everything in the morning before school, i.e. thumb, wash; first finger, eat; second finger, read Bible and notes; third finger, feed guinea pig; fourth finger, do hair. This helps her and she whizzes through and then has time to read. I could well do the same for myself. (Beth)

The idea is to put more and more onus for managing himself and his time on to the child. Therefore, if a mother finds that despite all her suggestions, she still has to nag, chivy, remind and do a great deal herself, she probably ought to stop everything and let the child be late, forget his book, and take the resulting detention, or whatever. This may cure the dawdler faster than anything else. (This *isn't* a good tactic with a child who dawdles because he hates school and is trying to put off the moment of getting there – only with a dreamy type who has been leaving it all to Mum, assuming she won't let him be late!)

THE WORLD ABOUT US

We can help our children to use their surroundings well and responsibly by making sure that they are not among the increasing number of 'litter louts' that there are about. Picnics should be meticulously cleared up, rubbish thrown into proper containers. As a family, you might like to consider joining one of the organisations that focuses on enjoying or taking care of beautiful buildings and wildlife. There are some very good environmental clubs for children and young people which run holiday schemes and other helpful programmes.

THE GOSPEL

Using God's gift of salvation and all that it brings responsibly, means receiving the gospel, living it out and sharing it with others. So we should encourage our young people to be involved in some form of Christian witness and outreach locally. I also believe that it's good for them to use some of their gifts of time and energy in serving the community in one way or another, through a local volunteer bureau, perhaps. To feel responsible for those who do not know the gospel and for those in need, is to follow in Jesus's footsteps.

PRIVILEGES AND RESPONSIBILITIES

It's very important to be generous, but not indulgent, parents.

> Some people we know have done everything for their children, e.g. they were always arranging parties, outings, different sorts of holidays entailing new equipment or gear, visits from friends, etc. In general, this was not appreciated but rather taken for granted.
>
> Another, poorer family we know is very different. The parents are kind and thoughtful, but encourage their children to stand on their own feet, while being ready to support as necessary. The rare dinner out for special occasions is fully appreciated and the parents are always highly spoken of by the children. (Rebecca)

A word to affluent parents

We can help our children to face life responsibly by *not* showering them with every material advantage, so that they never have to work, wait or save up for a thing, and end up disillusioned and looking for 'kicks' in dubious or dangerous ways. Instead we need to be wise in our giving and our withholding, and in making our children aware of how privileged they are and of their corresponding responsibilities.

10.

The human partners in Christian family life

Parents are human and all sorts of stresses and strains occur in the course of bringing up our children.

PARENTAL STRAINS AND STRESSES

True, a thriving baby is a glorious joy, so no wonder Wordsworth saw the young as trailing clouds of glory. But glory is not all they trail; they also bring broken nights, exhaustion, clutter, noise, disruption, worry, demands, problems . . . In a matter of months, a bonny bride can be reduced to a bleary-eyed zombie, too tired to dress properly, take care of the house or make love. Or else she can become engrossed with her children to such an extent that her husband feels jealous or neglected or both.

Another strain can arise through the wife feeling under-valued and frustrated, particularly when the children are small.

Sometimes I long for a satisfying, successful career. I am torn in half because I adore my children and would never want anyone else to take care of them – and yet I sometimes feel I will drown in washing and nappies.

Society, particularly the media, tends to denigrate the housewife's role and make her feel second-rate for not 'working', or else for not managing to look permanently glamorous, in a spotless dream house, surrounded by spotless dream children. The very term 'housewife' is inadequate; 'home manager' would be nearer the mark. (Harriet)

In theory, the husband and wife are 'one flesh', and it doesn't make sense for half of 'one flesh' to be more important – but in practice we have two human beings, one of whom is rewarded by pay packets, approval and promotions, while the other misses her career and work-mates horribly, and is ground down by routine and boring tasks, day in and day out. While she slogs on, her husband may well travel, go on stimulating courses, eat well, be surrounded by interesting colleagues, grow in confidence and have all his creature comforts provided. (Annabelle)

HELPING ONE ANOTHER THROUGH

Whole books have been written on parental strains and stresses and how husbands and wives can help one another through them (see the book list for a few of these titles). Here, I would like to stress four very important ways of strengthening the relationships between ourselves and our partners: sharing, reassurance, help and forgiveness.

Sharing feelings with each other and with God

Honesty with oneself, one's partner and God are absolutely crucial, but truth must always go hand in hand with love (Eph. 4:15). The purpose of sharing feelings is that we will inform and not wound one another. We *must* make time regularly to be alone with our partners in order to relax, talk and pray together.

Reassuring each other

What wives need to hear from their husbands, expressed in so many words, as well as in other ways is: 'You're a good wife and mother, and I'm proud of you!'

> Rex helps me so much by recognising that the job I am doing is hard and demanding, emotionally, physically and even mentally. Having to make decisions every day about different members of the family with their differing needs and wants is not easy. (Annabelle)

Also, husbands need to be reassured by wives that they are good husbands and fathers and that they are 'number one' in our lives after God.

Helping one another practically and sacrificially

Wives, submit to your husbands as to the Lord . . . Husbands, love your wives, just as Christ loved the church and gave himself up for her. (Eph. 5:22,25).
Submit to one another out of reverence for Christ. (Eph. 5:21).

I am convinced that bringing up the children needs to be seen as a joint responsibility.

> Rex's job is in the planning department and mine is the running of the house. The children are a joint job, so if Rex changes a dirty nappy, he is not doing me a favour, but if he washes up – he is. (Annabelle)

> We've always been friends and we tackle the children together. Ray has never told me to get on with it, or said, 'It's your job.' This has been a marvellous support. (Rebecca)

True, the wife will normally have most of the actual labour

(no pun intended!) but the responsibility should be shared and decisions talked over and made together.

The arrival of children will require sacrifices from *both* partners. The husband who tries to carry on as before, resents not having the 'pipe and slipper' treatment and expects the children to be 'tidied away' before he gets home, needs to take a good long look at the verses above and pray hard for agape-love. Learning to love his wife practically and unselfishly might mean taking a turn at attending to crying babies at night, involving himself in practical chores, and making sure she gets a regular break to pursue at least one of her interests. This sort of husband is less likely to have a discontented, exhausted wife.

On the other hand, wives need to take an active interest in their husband's work and put Ephesians 5 verse 22 into practice. Ideally, *both* should be learning to obey the previous verse and this will mean 'saying' to one another, 'How can I meet *your* needs?' not, 'How can you/why don't you meet mine?' And that's what real love is all about.

Keep forgiving each other and trying again

It must be hard to live with someone who is content with or refuses to admit his own evil. As it is, we both accept the fact that we are failures in God's sight and that we often fail each other so we confess our sins to him and admit them to one another, knowing that we will be forgiven, as we forgive. Like God, we can hate the sin while loving the sinner. (Annabelle)

'Do not let the sun go down while you are still angry, and do not give the devil a foothold.' (Eph. 4:26). This verse has to be the golden rule for Christian marriage and family life. (Cyril)

As we receive God's and one another's forgiveness, we can

start afresh, with no nagging sense of guilt. The amazing thing is that God uses us to our partners, our children and others, *just as we are*, while continuing to work in us. Among others in the Bible, Isaac, Jacob and David made colossal mistakes as fathers, but God moulded and used them and their children and grandchildren.

Many Bible leaders had strange family backgrounds which might have suggested that they would grow up as disasters, e.g. Abraham, Moses (brought up in Pharaoh's palace), Joseph (an insufferable child who needed lots of training), Samuel (separated early from his parents, and a poor father himself later on), David (possibly an after-thought), John the Baptist (who had very elderly parents). All these were accepted, used and changed by God. (Joan)

These examples mustn't, of course, cause us to think, 'Poor parenting doesn't matter, because God can use us and our children anyway!' But they can be a source of comfort when we fail through 'ignorance', 'weakness' or circumstances beyond our control, rather than through 'our own deliberate fault'. I would particularly wish it to be a source of hope to single parents deprived of the support of their partners and therefore that of the mothers or fathers of their children – through death, severe disease or disability, or divorce. Concerning divorced couples, it's far too simplistic and often cruel to suggest that it's six of one and half a dozen of the other; in a number of marriages – Christian ones among them – the arrival of the children uncovered the selfishness and immaturity of one partner, and the breakdown was caused by his or her refusal to face up to and take action about this. Once again, the word to the rest of us is: 'Judge not.'

The important thing is not to be crushed by failure or lose faith that things can change for the better. We must take note of the Jesuits' claim that a child given to them for the first seven years of his life would be moulded (to their way of thinking) for life: the first seven years are indeed vital, but it would be quite wrong to despair about achieving anything thereafter! It's never too late to try again, and people and situations can change dramatically when we see what is wrong and pray and plan for change with enough faith and determination.

11.

The four R's (a summary)

In a good Christian upbringing the four R's are very important, and I don't mean reading, writing and 'rithmetic, with a
fourth of that ilk, but reality, roots, reasons and relationships.
Reality. We need to see for ourselves, and help our children to
see, that having a biblical viewpoint is seeing things as they
really are, and living God's way is experiencing real life.
Jesus claimed to be the truth, and so Christianity is not just
the best way of life: it is life based on reality.
Roots. We want our children to develop roots that will grow
through all that is temporal into eternal realities; through
human love, acceptance and care, into the deeper, richer soil
of God's favour and purposes.
Reasons. Knowing God has a purpose in creation, our children can find compelling reasons for living, as well as some
explanation for the state of the world and for things that
happen day by day. Not that there are no mysteries or
unanswered questions – far from it. But we can show our
children that even in the absence of explanations, we can
trust God, knowing that he has his reasons and that these will
be made clear one day.
Relationships. We can also help them to see that the quality of
life is largely determined by how and whom we love and how
and by whom we are loved. Being loved by and loving God
brings out the very best in us and affects all other rela-

tionships and circumstances – and Jesus died to make all that possible.

The essential 'messages' that we want our children to receive about Christianity. If we can present Christianity to our children over the years, as the truth, as relevant to all life and relationships and as essentially *good news*, then we will have done our best, and the rest will be up to the Holy Spirit and to them.

Courage for Christian families

Bringing up our children to see and live life God's way is very demanding. But it's also exciting, as parents and children learn and grow together in homes where Jesus is Lord. Such homes are like beacons and havens to those who have lost their way in life or are being buffeted by its storms, and like salt in society. This makes them very unpopular with the 'prince of this world', and he and his followers are out to discredit and destroy Christian families. But Satan met his match long ago and need *never* have the upper hand, for: 'The one who is in you is greater than the one who is in the world.' (1 John 4:4).

And finally . . .

The farmer and his wife were sitting in the shade of a very special tree in their orchard – the one that had grown from the king's tiny brown pip, and was now able to withstand the storms of winter and to bear leaves, blossom and fruit in season.

'Been a lot of hard work, this tree,' said the farmer, thinking of the long days and nights of tending the young plant, watering it in drought, protecting it from frost, animals, blight . . .

'Go on, you've enjoyed every minute of it,' retorted his wife, patting his knee.

'Well, I wouldn't go that far,' said the farmer, with a laugh, 'but if you mean, "Was it worth it?" – of course it was.'

'Worth every minute,' his wife agreed.

12.

Workshop suggestions

In this section are ideas for workshop sessions with relevant lists and diagrams, which are also referred to in the previous text.

IDEAS FOR WORKSHOP SESSIONS FOR PARENTS

Some of the suggestions are suitable or could be adapted for prospective parents, engaged couples or young people.

- Write down all your partner's characteristics and qualities, while he/she does the same and then exchange pieces of paper and discuss what you have written.
- What are the characteristics of a truly Christian marriage? Think of its duration and exclusive quality, its purpose and aim, its pattern and power, its priorities and practice. Bible references for starters: 1 Cor. 6:17,19,20; 10:31; Mark 10:7–9; 1 Pet. 3:1–8; Gal. 5:13; Eph. 3:20; 5:21–33; Deut. 11:1.
- What are the differences between the way in which Christians and non-Christians would answer these questions: Whose children are they anyway? What are we bringing them up for? Who's responsible for bringing them up? What are the most important aspects of a good upbringing?

- What sort of behaviour and what attitudes and qualities does God want us to show to and encourage in our children? Group these, if possible, under spiritual, moral, mental, physical, emotional or social health. What does this tell you about God's attitude towards and interest in people? List the opposite kind of behaviour, qualities and attitudes. Do you need to take any action in the light of this teaching? Do your prayers need to be shaped or changed as a result of your study? Bible references for starters: Ps 119 (many verses); Prov. 11:1,13; 14:29; 15:19; 16:32; 25:19; Rom. 12:10; Eph. 4:25,28,31,32; 6:1,2; Phil. 3:14; 4:4; 1 Thess. 5:14; 2 Tim. 1:7; 2:22; Titus 3:2; Jas. 4:11; 1 Pet. 3:10.
- What does the Bible teach about discipline and training? Bible references: Prov. 3:11; 13:24; 19:18; 22:15; 23:13,14,15; 29:15,17; Eph. 6:4; Col. 3:21; Heb. 12:1–13.
- With your partner, write down the characteristics and qualities of each of your children and compare what you have written with the contents of pages 149 to 153. On the basis of this, write a prayer about each child, thanking God for every God-given characteristic and laying before him areas which need his wisdom and touch.
- Discuss the diagram on page 156. What other or different roots, branches and fruit would you have included (see also pages 55 to 98)?
- Discuss the suggestions on page 148, 154, 155 about what truths might be shared at the different ages. What other or different truths would you have included?
- Is your local church giving enough help to parents, children and families in general, by talks, discussions, counselling, etc? If not, how could you encourage the leaders to do so?
- Is your family too inward-looking? If so, discuss and implement ideas for being 'salt' and 'light' as a family to others – near and far.
- What are your strengths as a person? Is your family

getting the full benefit of them? If not, how could the situation be improved? For instance, if you are an understanding person and a good listener, how could you use these assets to serve your loved ones?

SOME BIBLICAL/CHRISTIAN TRUTHS THAT OUR UNDER-EIGHTS NEED TO KNOW

(The lists here and on pages 154, 155 are not intended to be comprehensive.)

- God created, knows all about and takes care of everyone and everything.
- He has shown us in the Bible how he wants us to live.
- Jesus, God's Son, was born as a human baby, grew up, lived life God's way, perfectly, was crucified, rose again, is alive today and will come back one day to be in charge of everyone and everything for ever.
- He wants to be our Saviour and Friend – forgiving us for the wrong things we do and helping us to live life, God's way.
- Living life God's way in our homes means inviting Jesus to be in charge, learning to love, obey, forgive and be forgiven, help, be grateful, do right and turn away from wrong, get on well together, face and overcome problems, be generous and welcoming.
- Living life God's way in our homes and anywhere else means growing more like Jesus – worshipping, loving, obeying, being friends with and learning more about God, and being kind to others.
- Living life God's way at school means obeying the teachers, doing our best, learning to do new things and to make friends with all sorts of people, and discovering more about God and all that he made, and his ways of working.
- Living life God's way on earth imperfectly is just getting ready for living life God's way perfectly in heaven.

Some characteristics of under-fives

(The diagrams here and on the following pages show only a selection of possible characteristics at the different stages.)

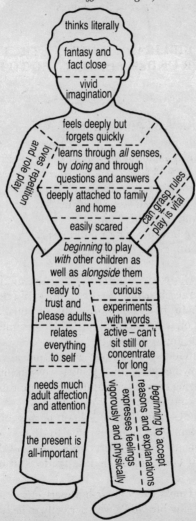

thinks literally

fantasy and fact close

vivid imagination

feels deeply but forgets quickly

loves repetition and role play

learns through *all* senses, by *doing* and through questions and answers

deeply attached to family and home

can grasp rules play is vital

easily scared

beginning to play *with* other children as well as *alongside* them

ready to trust and please adults

curious

experiments with words

relates everything to self

active – can't sit still or concentrate for long

needs much adult affection and attention

reasons and explanations

expresses feelings vigorously and physically

beginning to accept

the present is all-important

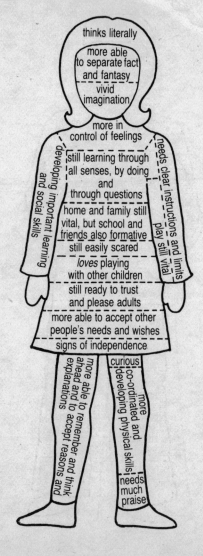

thinks literally

more able
to separate fact
and fantasy

vivid
imagination

more in
control of feelings

developing important learning
and social skills

still learning through
all senses, by doing
and
through questions

needs clear instructions and limits

play still vital

home and family still
vital, but school and
friends also formative

still easily scared

loves playing
with other children

still ready to trust
and please adults

more able to accept other
people's needs and wishes

signs of independence

more able to remember and think
ahead and to accept reasons and
explanations

curious

more
co-ordinated and
developing physical skills

needs
much
praise

Some characteristics of sevens to twelves

learning to reason

still tends to think literally and concretely

able to remember and think ahead

self-consciousness beginning

continuing to develop learning, social and creative skills

close to family still but friends and school very important too

needs reasons and explanations

starting to form judgments (not always correct ones!) about right/wrong, fairness/unfairness

ready to hero worship

curious

fluent

frank

loves play in a group with same-sex friends

growing more independent and responsible and more physical skills

greater co-ordination

responds well to projects/ challenges

eager for action and adventure

growing range of interests

needs to achieve and belong

Some characteristics of teenagers

aware of world

under pressure

able to reason and judge

idealistic

feels and shows a wide range of interests

developing considerably in knowledge and skills

moving away from dependence on parents and towards independence

developing deeper interests insecure, changeable

very self-aware

craves for acceptance – especially from friends and peers

wanting but fearing freedom, attention and responsibility

very aware of physical changes and often dissatisfied with personal appearance

experimenting in many ways to discover identity

interested in the opposite sex

testing all forms of authority

looking for answers

Some characteristics of young adults

(or older   teenagers)

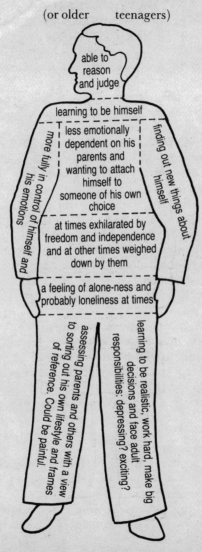

able to reason and judge

learning to be himself

less emotionally dependent on his parents and wanting to attach himself to someone of his own choice

finding out new things about himself

more fully in control of himself and his emotions

at times exhilarated by freedom and independence and at other times weighed down by them

a feeling of alone-ness and probably loneliness at times

assessing parents and others with a view to sorting out his own lifestyle and frames of reference. Could be painful.

learning to be realistic, work hard, make big decisions and face adult responsibilities; depressing? exciting?

SOME BIBLICAL CHRISTIAN TRUTHS
THAT OUR JUNIORS
(SEVENS TO ELEVENS/TWELVES)
NEED TO KNOW

- God is great and powerful, just and fair, loving and good.
- He wants to be 'number one' in our lives, otherwise he won't be able to give us, make us, show us or teach us all he wants to.
- When we ask Jesus to be our Saviour and Friend, his Holy Spirit can start giving us, making us, showing us and teaching us all those things, little by little.
- He will go on doing those things if we want him to, ask him to, keep obeying, praying, worshipping, reading our Bibles and learning from other Christians.
- Living God's way is an adventure (read or tell stories of Christians who live adventurously and courageously in different ways to illustrate this), and it's the way he planned we should live for our own good, as well as for other people's.
- God has plans for each life, which we can discover and fit in with or ignore and go our own way.
- Satan, God's enemy, has quite different plans, and many people today are fitting in with them, just as they have always done – which is why there is so much sin and sadness in and around us.
- Whatever we do and choose brings consequences, so choosing to live life God's way leads to one sort of life, and choosing to live Satan's or our own way leads to another: the choice is ours.
- We have to start learning to see everything we have and are, and all that happens to us, from Jesus's point of view, and to act accordingly.
- This will not be easy because many people don't see things from this viewpoint, but Jesus will help and bless us.

SOME BIBLICAL/CHRISTIAN TRUTHS
THAT OUR TEENAGERS NEED TO KNOW

Different series on the following would be helpful:

- Basic Christian doctrines (work of Holy Spirit – important; also – Jesus).
- Relationships with oneself (personality/emotions/worry/fear/the tongue/self-control).
- Relationships with others (boy-girl/marriage/parents/other Christians/non-Christians).
- Practical Christian living (the Christian and work/guidance/the community/the world at large/sects and cults/evil/morality/the supernatural/leisure/the media/creativity and the arts).
- Christianity in practice (Christian testimony from people who are seeing God at work and who are living out their faith in various situations).
- Bible Studies (how to understand and apply it; its accuracy; the fulfilments of prophecy).

Feeding in the Christian counter-culture is essential and the following are important here:

- True riches are spiritual, not material, and true goodness must be inward, outward and God-ward.
- True love is strong, sacrificial, unconditional and unstoppable – and only God's Holy Spirit can produce it, and other qualities, in us.
- True freedom and joy come as by-products of loving and obeying God (generally – i.e. growing like Jesus, taking care of the world, and sharing the good news, and specifically – i.e. in relation to the work we do and all the other decisions and details of our daily lives), and loving and serving others for his sake.
- Real life is Christ-centred, not self-centred, and involves humility and constant forgiveness and help from God.
- There is a spiritual war raging and we need spiritual armour for it.

- All events are sent or allowed by God and can be opportunities to know, trust, love or serve him better.

Roots and fruit

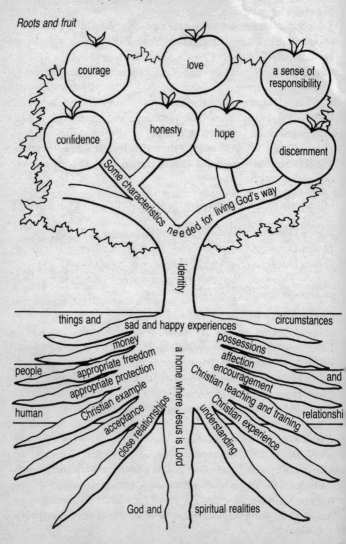

courage

love

a sense of responsibility

confidence

honesty

hope

discernment

Some characteristics needed for living God's way

identity

things and

sad and happy experiences

circumstances

money

possessions

people

appropriate freedom

affection

appropriate protection

encouragement

a home where Jesus is Lord

Christian teaching and training

and

human

Christian example

Christian experience

relationshi

acceptance

understanding

close relationships

God and

spiritual realities

USEFUL BOOKS

On child development and care:
John Bowlby, *Child Care and the Growth of Love* (Penguin).
J. A. Hadfield, *Childhood and Adolescence* (Penguin).
H. Jolly, *Book of Child Care* (Allen & Unwin).
Penelope Leach, *Baby and Child* (Michael Joseph) (0–5 years).
K. Leech, *Youthquake* (Abacus).
D. W. Winnicott, *The Child, the Family and the Outside World* (Penguin).
(These must be read critically and rejected when they are unbiblical, but otherwise they contain a wealth of knowledge.)

On child development, care and training from Christian viewpoint:
James Dobson, *Dare to Discipline* (Kingsway).
James Dobson, *Discipline While You Can* (Kingsway).
James Dobson, *Hide or Seek* (Hodder & Stoughton).
James Dobson, *Preparing for Adolescence* (Kingsway) (addressed to adolescents).

On Christian marriage and family life:
James Dobson, *Man to Man About Woman* (Kingsway).
Elisabeth Elliot, *Let Me Be A Woman* (Hodder & Stoughton).
Ed. Edward England, *We Believe In Marriage* (Marshall).
Joyce Huggett, *Growing Into Love* (IVP).
Joyce Huggett, *Two Into One?* (IVP).
O. R. Johnston, *Who Needs the Family?* (Hodder & Stoughton).
Helen Lee, *Christian Marriage* (Mowbray).
Dr Shirley Leslie, *Children Growing up* (Scripture Union).
Marion Stroud, *I Love God and My Husband* (Victor Books) (helpful for those married to non-Christian partners).
Judson Swihart, *How Do You Say 'I Love You'?* (Kingsway).
Anne J. Townsend, *Marriage Without Pretending* (Scripture Union).

Anne Townsend, *Time For Change (How to grow with your teenager)* (Marshall).

Ann Warren, *Marriage in the Balance* (Kingsway).

John White, *Eros Defiled* (IVP).

John White, *Parents in Pain* (IVP).

God's Pattern for Enriched Living (Workshop One, Seminar Workshops for Women, PO Box 3039, Kent, Washington 98P31) (case histories, biblical principles and practical suggestions on improving family relationships).

On the child and the Church:

John Inchley, *All About Children* (Kingsway).

The Child in the Church (British Council of Churches, Report of the Working Party, 1976).

For parents who need to remind themselves of the Christian difference:

John R. W. Stott, *Christian Counter-Culture* (IVP).

John V. Taylor, *Enough is Enough* (SCM Press).

A. N. Triton, *Whose World?* (IVP).

On Christian sex education:

Mary Kehle, *You're Nearly There (Christian Sex Education For Ten-To-Teens)* (Pickering & Inglis).

Susan Schaeffer Macauley, *Something Beautiful From God* (Marshall).

To help with Bible reading/family prayers:

Notes for all ages are available from Scripture Union; also *Time For the Family* (four magazines) for use in family prayers.

HIDE OR SEEK

James Dobson

An epidemic of inferiority is raging throughout our society. From the moment children enter the world they are subjected to a value system which reserves respect and esteem for only a select few. Those who fail to measure up – particularly in the areas of intelligence and beauty – are left with feelings of inadequacy.

Dr. Dobson asserts that only Christian values free us from the tyranny of self and offer dignity and respect to every human being. Through this better way, children can be given the courage to *seek the best*, rather than *hide in fear and sorrow*.

STRAIGHT TALK TO MEN
AND THEIR WIVES

James Dobson

'If families are to survive the incredible stresses and dangers they now face, it will be because husbands and fathers provide loving leadership in their homes, placing their wives and children at the highest level on their system of priorities.'

A warm, intensely personal, often amusing account of the way family relationships can and should work.